D0753075

# A Bite Off Mama's Plate ◆◆◆

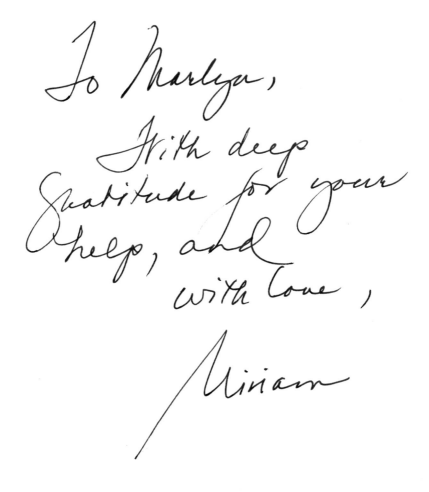

To Marlyn,
With deep
gratitude for your
help, and
with love,

Miriam

# A *Bite* off
# Mama's Plate

*Mothers' and Daughters' Connections through Food*

Miriam Meyers

**Bergin & Garvey**
Westport, Connecticut • London

**Library of Congress Cataloging-in-Publication Data**

Meyers, Miriam, 1941–
    A bite off Mama's plate : mothers' and daughters' connections through food /
    Miriam Meyers.
        p.   cm.
    Includes bibliographical references and index.
    ISBN 0–89789–788–9 (alk. paper)
    1. Food habits—United States—History.   2. Women—United States—Social
conditions.   3. Mothers and daughters—United States.   4. Cookery, American—
History.   5. Dinners and dining—United States—History.   I. Title.
GT2853.U5M48   2001
394.1'2'0820973—dc21          2001018478

British Library Cataloguing in Publication Data is available.

Library of Congress Catalog Card Number: 2001018478
ISBN: 0–89789–788–9

First published in 2001

Bergin & Garvey, 88 Post Road West, Westport, CT 06881
An imprint of Greenwood Publishing Group, Inc.
www.greenwood.com

Printed in the United States of America

The paper used in this book complies with the
Permanent Paper Standard issued by the National
Information Standards Organization (Z39.48–1984).

10 9 8 7 6 5 4 3 2 1

*To Mama, with ever-increasing appreciation.*

# Contents

# *Preface*

*A Bite Off Mama's Plate* is a book built on the generosity of women. Hundreds of women (and some special men) helped me, and in myriad ways—with the research, with ideas, with ongoing support of many kinds. It is impossible to name them all, but some must be acknowledged. The women who attended the focus groups and those who interviewed with me in family groups helped build the foundation; many are named in the book, if only by first name. Alice Deakins told me from the outset, "You have a book." Thank you, Alice.

Nancy Eustis, Fancher Wolfe, and Ed Mack, survey research experts, evaluated and helped me improve my survey instrument. To those who distributed it around the country—and those who completed it—I owe a debt, especially Barbara Arnett, Jackie Bartley, Nancy Black, Diannah Carrington, Alice Deakins, Jackie DeHon, Caroline Dunlap, Mary Ann Ecklund, Marje Jaasma, Frances Jeffries, Carol Lacey, Roz Miller, Maggie Patterson, Addie Sayers, Anita Taylor, Milt Thomas, Bertie Wells, and the amazing women of the Minneapolis downtown YWCA's morning water aerobics class.

At Metropolitan State University, I had the assistance of the library staff—the tireless Kim Scannell, Adela Peskorz, Marty Swenson, and Sage Holben—in obtaining hundreds of articles and books; copy center and mysterious-machines-expert Joy Harris, with work-study students Maria Kravchik, Ramona Peterson, Margarita Tchaldarian, Tookie Sanger, and Emmanuelle Caillet; and Lisa McMahon, who gave cheerful assistance from the beginning. The extraordinary Tim Dunsworth of the institutional research office worked with the statistical data far more generously, ethically, and intelligently than I could have hoped for. Donna Paul and Jessica Thomson gave invaluable help in coding and processing the surveys. Leah Harvey, as colleague, dean, and academic vice president, has always helped by believing in my work, and Fred Kirchhoff, my current dean, has cheered me on every step of the way, helping to fuel the fire. University professional development grants helped me pay costs associated with the work. The women of Metro State who responded to my survey showed their typical spirit by writing more answers to open questions than any other single group. I am in their debt for this and more.

Jane Garry and Jane Lerner, my editors, showed enthusiasm for seeing the book in print and helped in many ways to make it happen, part of what kept me going. Many women of the Organization for the Study of Communication, Language, and Gender provided assistance and moral support. Catherine Warrick, my long-time colleague and beloved friend, applied her uncommon intelligence and wisdom to reading and commenting on drafts of the manuscript. It was she who urged me not to underplay the importance of the family dinner, and for that I am especially grateful. Diana Riehl, my soul-sister for 35 years, whose judgment I always seek and trust, helped in ways too numerous to count. Nancy Eustis listened cheerfully to endless details of the book's progress and still offered help. What a friend. All my friends, in fact, have shown amazing forbearance and helpfulness. Barbara and Robert Arnett, sister- and brother-in-more-than-law, and dear friends Jean and Malcolm Clark gave us the use of their vacation homes as lovely, quiet places to write, walk, and talk about the book.

The other half of "us" is my partner of 34 years, Chet Meyers. More than spouse, he is best friend, constant and frank critic-teacher (he occasionally wrote "Urp" in the margins of drafts, then explained in ways that led to improvements), and patient, patient, patient companion during the years I put into the book.

Without my mother, of course, it never would have happened. She would be pleased, if surprised, that I wrote a book about food.

# *A Note to the Reader*

The Reference Notes following Chapter 8, arranged by chapter and page number, document sources of information used in the book, elaborate on certain points, give further information on original research reported in the chapters, and suggest further reading on some subjects for those interested. Complete publication information on sources named in the text and in the notes follows in References.

# 1

## "Thinking Back through Our Mothers": Introduction

A year or so after my mother died, I visited her grave in the beautiful old Atlanta cemetery where she lies. Driving there from the airport, I stopped at a weedy vacant lot where I caught sight of a man preparing hickory-smoked barbecue in a drum and selling it from a modest shed. A few minutes later, sitting on the ground beside Mama's grave, I found myself "talking" with her as I enjoyed a messy-but-delicious lunch. I knew if she'd been able to eat with me, we'd have been talking about that barbecue pork sandwich and coleslaw—and relishing it. Enjoying a meal at her grave was the best possible way to celebrate the memory of my mother.

That graveside picnic was just one of many times I've remembered Mama over food. Fairly regularly now, especially when I am alone for lunch, I fix myself a meal of eggs, grits, and coffee, and sit down to "be" with her. If I have ham in the house, I grill some of that and make red-eye gravy. A meal like this, laden as it is with both fat and Southernness, is completely foreign to most of my friends in the Upper Midwest, where I now live, but it is soul-satisfying food to me. In the decade since her death, I feel closest to my mother when I sit down before a meal I know she would enjoy. It's communion. As one woman puts it, "the way to begin to heal . . . is to be connected to her spirit." And there is no better way to do this, in my case, than to eat something good and think about how Mama would enjoy it.

I have long had this strong bond with my mother through food, though I never really thought seriously about it until 1994. That year, I viewed Laura Esquivel's film *Like Water for Chocolate* with a group of women who study and teach the connections between communication and gender. We were, during that particular session, exploring that universal, complex connection, the mother-daughter relationship. Esquivel's compelling film, portraying in an unforgettable way the power of food in families, helped me see in a new way my own connections with my family through food—and my mother's part in that. Members of my family led very different lives and often disagreed with one another on matters of importance to us. Yet we came together eagerly, and with genuine enjoyment, around a meal. At the center of this enjoyment, of course, was Mama, whose delight in food and whose knowledge and skill in planning and preparing food blessed not only her family and friends but countless others who benefited from her work in the food service industry.

I related all this to my colleagues following our viewing of the film, and a lively discussion ensued. They thought I should look more seriously into women's connections with their mothers through food. They saw the opportunity for new insights into women's communication. The idea appealed to me, but I set it on the back burner (to use a cooking metaphor), given other commitments. The next year, the group met again. What, they asked, had I done to advance the work on mothers and daughters and food? The energy these women brought to the topic—their stories, their encouragement to pursue the idea, their offers of help—made me see there was something here that demanded attention. Since that day, moral support, material and people resources, and energy to pursue the project have come my way continually. There is a rightness to the work that has propelled it forward.

As I began to look at published work on mothers and daughters, I was surprised to find no explorations of the varied ways food connects us. Aside from the literature on eating disorders such as anorexia nervosa and bulimia, our national obsession with dieting, and the mother's implication in those problems ("among the crimes laid at [the mother's] doorstep"), one is hard pressed to find serious discussion of the role—especially any *positive* role—food plays in the mother-daughter relationship. This struck me as exceedingly odd, given the omnipresence of food in human life, women's assignment of responsibility for family food across cultures, and a body of research showing that the mother-daughter relationship is "mutual and interdependent . . . , rewarding . . . and close. . . ."

It is to this void that I direct this book. The book explores a range of connections women in families have through food. While I do not deny or suppress such problematic connections as disordered eating, I contend that they receive considerable attention. Were a time capsule containing the serious mother-daughter literature of the last few decades to be opened by a future generation, the inescapable conclusion would be that the mother-daughter food connection in our time is primarily a troubled and troubling one. What I have heard from hundreds of women, since embarking on this study, convinces me that this is not a full and, therefore, not an accurate picture and that the imbalance in the literature needs redress. I agree with Terri Apter, who writes that what remains unwritten about mothers and daughters "is the story about how connection between [them] . . . remains a strength," and I hope to demonstrate the part food plays in that connection.

It is worth considering, though, why it is that broader, especially more positive, food connections have not been fully explored. One reason may be the American tendency to focus on problems. "If it's not broken, don't fix it" is the other side of "If it's broken, fix it." We are a people who like to fix what's wrong. We do have eating disorders, and the problem is reaching epidemic proportions, according to some public health researchers. Anthropologist Sidney Mintz points out an underlying factor when he writes of our "compulsive concern with the way the body is seen and assessed." Since, as women, we learn from our mothers as well as from our peers and other teachers, it is inevitable that some social critics and analysts of eating problems will trace those problems to the mother. *Like Mother, Like Daughter*, thus, is the name of one book on disordered eating and *My Mother Made Me Do It* another. Sadly, the "not-broken" part of the mother-daughter relationship through food is usually relegated to the food section of the local newspaper, to the pages of so-called "women's magazines," and to episodes in fiction and autobiography. It may seem too commonplace to deserve serious attention.

But there are other factors. The nineteenth-century view of the ideal woman, with its elaborate physical and emotional demands, continues to haunt twenty-first century women. Catherine Manton has shown how the industrial revolution, and the domestic science movement with its accompanying marketing efforts, instilled in American women uneasiness not only about their own physical appearance and health, but about following family traditions or their own instincts in feeding themselves and others. She suggests further that American women's feelings about themselves in relation to food have become increasingly negative in the last 150 years.

During the decade of the fifties, for example, perhaps the height of efforts to glorify a style of homemaking that can only be described as strenuous, women spent increased time in housekeeping, despite the explosion of household appliances and gadgets intended to make their work more efficient. Mechanization of the kitchen did not fulfill its promise of decreasing time spent in housekeeping, then, due to escalating expectations about what was necessary or desirable. The idealization of perfectly clean homes and perfectly cooked and arranged food thus constituted oppression for most women, especially as the demands of life multiplied and most women added work outside the home to that inside the home. (As a friend said recently, "How can we relax when there's Martha Stewart?")

Two-thirds of all American women—and about the same proportion of women who are mothers—are now in the labor force. Yet historians show that women's entry into the labor force did not change "the relationship of women—as daughters, wives, and mothers—to their families." In spite of the increasing willingness of some men to participate in the work of homemaking, it is still women who bear the brunt of that labor. As one researcher observes, "The allocation of work in the home continues to be shaped by deeply ingrained ideas about the roles of the sexes." Studies of adults' use of time have found that men cook less than one-tenth as often as women and that, indeed, women spend twice as much time overall as men on so-called "maintenance" activities, such as cleaning, shopping, cooking and housework.

Even when men involve themselves in cooking, women have been shown to retain responsibility for food management. Planning, acquiring and preparing food has thus become a burden for some women, even those for whom such activities might be pleasurable in a different set of circumstances.

A good deal of effort has been expended during the last four decades, then, to help us shed the legacy of nineteenth-century views of women, to undo the damage of the fifties' messages about appropriate home care and food preparation, and to examine and critique gender roles, including the assignment of food-related tasks to women. It is therefore completely understandable that some women object to linking women and food again. When Arlene Voski Avakian solicited contributions to her anthology, *Through the Kitchen Window: Women Explore the Intimate Meanings of Food and Cooking*, she received this response from a scientist she appealed to for a contribution: "Haven't we had enough of women being viewed through the kitchen window? . . . I cannot help but feel that it is self-indulgent to put together a U.S. collection on women and food, when women and feminists are confronting so many problems and engaged in such struggles in this country and elsewhere."

I understand such a reaction, but I cannot share it. For one thing, the place of food in women's lives was traditionally ignored by scholars. Indeed, it is only recently that serious study of food in general has blossomed, in spite of its capacity to shed important light on the way society functions. One anthropological study of eating, in fact, asserts that "[c]ultural traits, social institutions, national histories, and individual attitudes cannot be entirely understood without an understanding also of how these have meshed with our varied and peculiar modes of eating." Sidney Mintz believes food was largely neglected until recently as a serious area of study (especially in developed societies) by other anthropologists because women did most of the "food work" and anthropologists, mostly men, "didn't find such matters especially interesting." In other fields as well, "women's work" has been ignored and not considered a "serious intellectual interest." Even sociological studies of family life traditionally ignored "cooking, eating and clearing up"—an unfortunate exclusion, given that, as recent food historians point out, food habits, values, and attitudes "[help] to fashion the peculiar tone and direction of a society."

Across academic scholarship, the story is the same. Philosophers now studying food attribute other scholars' indifference to their tendency "to privilege questions about the rational, the unchanging and eternal, and the abstract and mental; and to denigrate questions about embodied, concrete, practical experience." Since food and eating are all about embodiment, concreteness, practice, *and* experience, clearly they would be excluded from the realm.

The traditional neglect of food as a serious topic for study is now turning around. I knew of little scholarly work on food before starting my own investigation. Many books and articles, written from many perspectives, have appeared, or come to my attention, since. Some offer an opportunity to strengthen our knowledge of women's contributions to our common life. What we learn about the place of food in the mother-daughter relationship can only improve our understanding of those contributions and foster respect for women. Rather than suppressing women's contributions to food and eating, with its "astonishing, at times even terrifying, importance," I hope, rather, that bringing them to light will help build a complete picture. An aspect of life in which women have so prominent a place, food is simply too important a domain to be ignored. As Luce Giard notes, "with their high degree of ritualization and their strong affective investment, culinary activities are for many women of all ages a place of happiness, pleasure, and discovery. Such life activities demand as much intelligence, imagination, and memory as those traditionally held as superior, such as music and weaving." I would add that many women have invested themselves in food-related activities to positive ends, and I offer this book in part as a tribute to their work.

A final note about the book's focus. I have intentionally concentrated on connections *women* have through food in families—especially mothers and daughters. There is no intention to deny the strong connections men have through food with family members. Clearly they have such connections, and, increasingly, they have a role in providing meals for the family. Nor do I want to suggest that *all* women in families have strong connections through food; some do not. Everything in this book is not true for *every* mother and daughter, nor is there anything "wrong" with mothers and daughters to whom it does not apply. I focus on mothers and daughters because the need presented itself to me;

then one opportunity after another encouraged me to pursue the work; and it has taken on personal significance for me—as a way to remember and honor my own mother. Finally, I focus on North American mothers and daughters, though much of what I write no doubt applies to mothers and daughters in other places, and some parts to those virtually everywhere.

The book elaborates some of the themes I drew from reading and listening to women's reflections and through research into related scholarly and popular literature. Recipes contributed by research participants are sprinkled throughout the book. Chapter 2 places the study of mothers' and daughters' connections through food in the context of the family and the larger community. In Chapter 3, I explore the various ways food serves as the occasion for, and topic of, mother-daughter communication. Chapter 4 examines women's learning of food-related skills, the mother's place in that, and the influence daughters bring to bear on their mothers in the food arena. Food for the circumstances of life is the subject of Chapter 5. Chapter 6 details the ways food ensures continuity across generations of women in families, while Chapter 7 features messages about life women receive observing their mothers' approach to food. Chapter 8 closes the book with testimony to the strength and inspiration women draw from their mothers, and other women of history, through food. "Reference Notes," indicating sources used in the chapters, as well as additional information, and "References" follow Chapter 8 and offer the reader help in following up on topics of interest.

A word is in order on how women who are the sources of stories and comments are identified in the text. To avoid tedious repetition of source details, I adopted the following pattern: For each respondent to the survey I conducted, I use typically two of the following four selected details: current state of residence, childhood state (or country) of residence, age, and occupation—"a 68-year-old retired CPA." By contrast, participants in the interviews I conducted, and other individual women contributing to the book's contents (nonanonymously), are identified typically by first name ("Rhonda"), or, if other contributors share that name, by first name and initial ("Joanne N.," "Joanne R."). Sources not generated by my own research are identified, by page number of the text, in "Reference Notes."

Vivien Nice writes that some women "are beginning to 'think back through our mothers' in the true sense of valuing the strengths and creativity, *however expressed*, of the mothers who gave birth to us" (italics added). Having heard the voice of women contributing to this book, and having experienced the relish with which they joined in developing its content, offering hundreds of stories and comments to help it along, I know that food and its place in the mother-daughter relationship is a subject more than worth cracking open. I've learned that, despite some warnings to the contrary, women are willing, even eager, to reflect on their relationship to their mothers through food. I now invite readers to enjoy with me the richness of women's reflected experience.

# 2

# "A Subject of the Greatest Importance": Food and the Family

As I write these words, my summer garden is alive with birds feeding their young and teaching them how to find their own food. These bird families seem busy with food most of their active hours, the parents searching for it, rendering it fit for tiny mouths, then delivering it; the little ones crying out impatiently, then gobbling greedily whatever is brought to them.

The scene reminds me just how fundamental to life food is. We need food to survive and grow. "Without at least minimal access to food and water, we die," in the words of one anthropologist. Thus, like the birds, we occupy ourselves obtaining, preparing, and consuming it.

But food means more than physical survival. Nothing demonstrates this better than a very special cookbook published in 1996, more than 50 years after it was written. *In Memory's Kitchen: A Legacy from the Women of Terezín* tells one of the most poignant stories of the twentieth century. The book features a collection of recipes written by women at Terezín, which has been described as "the anteroom to Auschwitz," in what is now Czechoslovakia. As she lay dying of malnutrition, Mina Pächter pressed the hand-sewn volume onto a friend and asked him to get it to her daughter who had escaped to Palestine. It took twenty-five years for Anny

Stern to receive the package and another twenty-seven for it to see publication.

*In Memory's Kitchen* is not a conventional cookbook. Its editor, Cara De Silva, writes that many of the recipes are incomplete and incorrect, thus bearing witness to the appalling conditions under which the women were living. The creation of the cookbook, she says, "was an act of psychological resistance, forceful testimony to the power of food to sustain us, not just physically but spiritually."

Food is who we are in the deepest sense, and not because it is transformed into blood and bone. Our personal gastronomic traditions—what we eat, the foods and foodways we associate with the rituals of childhood, marriage, and parenthood, moments around the table, celebrations—are critical components of our identities. To recall them in desperate circumstances is to reinforce a sense of self and to assist us in our struggle to preserve it.

The contribution foodways make to our sense of self is enormous, indeed, and they emanate from the family and the larger community. It is there, then, that we begin to look at mothers' and daughters' connections through food.

In her novel *Like Water for Chocolate*, Laura Esquivel treats in an unforgettable way the magical things that can happen through and around meals. So central is the role of food in her family that Tita, family cook *extraordinaire*, reflects that it might have been the smell of the Christmas rolls she loved so much that "made her decide to trade the peace of ethereal existence in Mama Elena's belly for life as her daughter, in order to enter the De la Garza family and share their delicious meals and wonderful sausage."

Though the power of food and eating is rarely experienced as spectacularly in most people's lives as in Esquivel's characters'— releasing their long-repressed sexual desires, or making them weep so that their tears run down the stairs—clearly, it functions within families in special ways. Like Esquivel's De la Garzas, many families find that, when they can agree on little else as a family, food forges a link between them, providing a topic for conversation and an activity to enjoy together—enthusiastically.

The family connection reflects a broader one that people achieve through food. One expert in public health, psychology, and psychiatry believes it is important to see food as more than a fuel or nutrient, since "it is used in the culture, policy, ritual, and religion of a society." Thus the significance of food in our cultural celebrations and the ancient stories they reenact. As Lynne Rossetto Kasper, food writer and host of the syndicated radio program *The Splendid Table* notes, "Food is a huge part of our spirituality." Other contemporary observers agree and emphasize the soundness of the link between food and spirit. Thomas Moore says that "preparing food is like alchemy," and our souls need the magic of such transformations. And transformations they are, as films like *Babette's Feast* and *My Dinner with André* demonstrate. Pharmacologist Candace Pert suggests that the digestive system is more than a processing center for food. It is also "a major emotional center—a site for the soul." She describes food as "a transition between the emotional and the physical. You eat, and the food turns into your body. . . . By nature, it's spiritual." Perhaps it is not surprising, then, that table grace, "the most ubiquitous religious practice in contemporary North America," is related to food.

Food plays a central role in religious practice. Anthropologist Sidney Mintz remarks that "the entanglements of food with religion, with both belief and sociality, are particularly striking." This fact is apparent to anyone involved in American religious communities. Recent research on the place of food in mainline Protestant Christian churches, for example, reveals how important a feature it has been in those churches and how, over the past three decades, the emphasis in "sociality" has shifted from sociability to social responsibility. Many churches now eschew feeding themselves. Instead, they feed the hungry, operate food shelves, and scrutinize their foodways to adjust them to a new ethical standard.

Christian holy communion itself points to the essentially spiritual nature of eating together as a community, as does Jewish Passover, the tradition it comes from. It is said that on the road to Emmaus, the risen Jesus was known to his followers *only as they shared something to eat*: ". . . their eyes were opened, and they recognized Jesus. . . ." The implications of the story are worth pondering, regardless of one's religious persuasion. There is power in sharing food together that makes us truly recognizable, *knowable*, to one another.

# COMING TOGETHER AROUND MEALS

When I took my first teaching job after finishing college, I moved to a state where I knew no one. Through the generosity of my principal's secretary, I boarded for a time with her family. The evening meal was so much a part of my sense of an organized and civilized life that Alma Rich's dinners, and the communion they entailed, made her house a home for me. She worked all day, just as I did, but prepared a home-cooked meal for four every night. The Riches' dinner table provided a break from the hard work and cares of the day and an opportunity to catch up on the lives of others in the household. Dinner required the four of us to let our individual worries and struggles drop away so that we could be fit company, engaging in pleasant conversation. It took us, in short, out of our separate worlds and into community. In retrospect, I realize what a gift these dinners were.

## The Family Dinner

Food's central place in a common life manifests itself clearly in the belief in the importance of the family dinner—"our most civilizing ritual," in the words of Marion Cunningham. Women express this belief in a variety of ways. Survey respondents write of "the strength of a family that eats meals together" and dinner time as "really family time." Kate L. noted in an interview that it was "really important" in her family home not only "for everyone to sit down around a table, [but to] stay there for the whole meal." No television was allowed. "Good conversation goes with dinner," writes a forty-eight-year-old educator. An Oklahoma college student writes of the best thing about her relationship with her mother through food in five words: "We always had Sunday dinner."

Research showing that family interactions concentrate more around dinnertime than at any other time confirms the soundness of comments linking dining and family welfare. Family life authority William Doherty, in fact, recommends "family meals as the best place to begin the process of becoming more intentional as a family." Most often such meals will be in the evening, but Doherty suggests that weekend meals, such as Sunday brunch, can serve if common evening meals are not possible. If there is *no* common family meal, other arrangements must be made to insure time for interaction normally accomplished in that setting. Given their circumstances, some families must find alternatives. But it is hard to imagine a ritual that can accomplish as much at one time as the family meal manages to do.

Two women in their fifties explain the meaning evening meals in the family hold for them. One, a Texas business owner, says her good memories of her childhood home are not of the food so much as "being together and slowing down, settling into the nest for the evening." Another, a New Jersey sales representative, learned from her mother that "sharing good food and meals brings people together in a warm and loving atmosphere. . . . After working outside of the home all day, it is comforting to come home and smell delicious aromas and be able to sit down and have a hot meal."

The value of meals as a social time and a time for bonding the family came up again and again in interviews and surveys as women reflected on their experience. One woman described the family dinner as "a kind of communion." Barbara S. emphasized that the focus is not so much on food consumption but on the fact that "everyone comes together around the common table, and that's the *only* time when people of the different generations come together, in one place, and engage in a common activity." She went on to say that now, with her parents and siblings (and the siblings' children) scattered widely around the country, the extended family gathers around a common table mainly when they travel to vacation at their lake home. In her childhood home, though, it was an evening meal, "a major time of ritual. . . . When we were young . . . we would read. We read *Charlotte's Web*, chapter by chapter, at the dinner table. . . ." Barbara's memory of family dinners focuses on collectivity.

A number of women emphasized the importance of dinner conversation for building and even healing the family. Parents who struggle to keep the ritual going acknowledge that it isn't always easy. Jenny admits that her insistence on having dinner together "drives my kids crazy. It's hard to keep making that happen." But, in fact, her children *do* talk with one another, even when they insist they have "nothing to say. . . . They're quite amazed that we do have things to talk about!" Kevlyn remarked how being together at the table can heal rifts as well: "With three teenagers in the house, there can be all kinds of controversies and all kinds of arguments. . . . We may not always have large dinners, but we always have a large Sunday dinner. And there can be those who aren't speaking to each other coming to the Sunday table. . . . Usually by the time we sit down and start having our meal, there's visiting going on." Kevlyn's mother Beverly echoed the "tremendous advantage" afforded by family meals: "No matter how bad the fight, how deep the wound, you can feed 'em, and that heals."

Coming together as a family specifically around meals makes perfect sense in light of what we know about the intersection of food and feeling. That is, when we are eating, we tend to feel better than at other times. Psychological studies of people's feelings during the activities of everyday life suggest that "a graph of a person's level of happiness during the day resembles the profile of the Golden Gate Bridge across San Francisco Bay, *with the high points corresponding to mealtimes*" (italics added). Families who come together at mealtimes capitalize on the highs in our daily rhythms.

Besides offering a setting to strengthen family bonds, against the tide of "slowly diminishing connection, meaning, and community" evident to observers of modern family life, the family dining table provides an important place for children to learn. Recent work by Ellen Galinsky of the Work and Family Institute names as one of eight critical parenting skills "providing routines and rituals to make life predictable and create positive neural patterns in developing brains." In studying children's communication, researchers find that extended mealtime conversation can increase young children's vocabulary and prepare them to learn to read. Research concentrating on high school students demonstrates how family commensality and nutrition, both tied to family meals, correlate positively with young people's academic performance.

Moreover, children learn family stories, manners, and consideration for others, among other things, at mealtime. One study of middle-class families at dinner—all of which included a kindergarten age child—showed that "discipline" was the second largest category of conversation topics, a sign of how central at the family table is children's behavior development.

Anthropologists Peter Farb and George Armelagos enumerate some of what children may learn at the table:

A meal in North America or Europe involves certain assumptions having to do with the time of day, the seating arrangements, and the sequence of the courses. Most families also observe certain rules: Who sits where is based either on status or on habit; there is a restriction on moving about; conversations are expected to be free from disgusting topics; and usually there is a prohibition of other activities (such as speaking on the telephone). A meal presupposes certain minimal requirements about the food itself. A serving of baked beans and coffee does not qualify in North America as a proper lunch or dinner. . . .

In fact, children learn how to choose food at the table. A recent Harvard Medical School study of children's dining patterns and food intake found that eating a better diet is a benefit associated with family dinner. Mintz adds manual dexterity to the list of things learned at the table; child development experts Dreyer and Dreyer add a variety of "roles, rules, and values," as well as sensuous enjoyment and expression of feeling. So researchers from a range of perspectives support what many of us know in our bones—that meals serve as a focal point for learning and socialization. And both continue until children leave the family home, if conditions are right.

One member of a large family voiced her concern about what youngsters miss when they are not truly present at the table because they're "plugged in" to music, or listening to, or for, other electronic devices.

It's not okay. They [have an opportunity to] hear the family story. It's not just the current gathering that they're missing. Teenagers can live without getting together with their aunts and uncles, but it's all the stories that are shared. . . . I believe they're missing a critical sense of their own link into a larger extended family. . . . they're missing nuances of how to be when they grow up. . . . These are rites of passage. The family stories and family humor are their connections. [The elders] will be gone, and they won't have absorbed them, and nobody can replace that. Nobody can sit down with them later in life and say "Do you remember the story about . . . ?" It loses something in the translation. A lot of that happens around meals . . . , as well as traditions that have built up. I know it's hard for kids. But just being around, they'll absorb the stories and a way of being.

## Extended Family Dinners

The foregoing comments about what children miss when they are absent from meals, physically or otherwise, come from a woman's experience in her extended family, rather than her nuclear family. Extended family gatherings typically take place around meals. Women sometimes write about these gatherings, and their mother's place in them, responding to the open survey question "The best thing about my relationship with my mother through food is. . . ." A Virginia college student, for example, appreciates that her mother "brought the family, especially the extended family, together." A forty-seven-year-old administrator writes of how her mother has invited her and her children for dinner once a week for the past decade.

Many women learn from their mothers, in the words of one fifty-six-year-old, that "good, plentiful food is an important part of family events." Ninety-two percent of survey respondents agree that food is an important part of extended family gatherings. These meals may take place in restaurants (55 percent say they "sometimes" do), but 43 percent say their families never have such meals in restaurants.

When I was a youngster, most extended family meals took place at the home of the great-aunt who served as surrogate mother to my mother from her sixth year forward. On Sunday, the spreads at Aunt Clifford's were, not surprisingly, much like my mother's during that era. We might have fried chicken, biscuits with gravy, creamed white corn, fried okra, and a plate of sliced tomatoes— a spread now out of vogue, even in many Southern homes, but delicious and heady back then. After the large midday meal, the women would cover the food, still in its serving dishes, with a cloth, leaving it on the table. Following an afternoon of visiting, the food would be uncovered and we would have a light meal, choosing what we wanted from the bowls and platters. Far from seeing this "second round" as dreary leftovers, we viewed it as a chance to enjoy again what had been so tasty earlier.

In my interview with Judy and her daughters, Natalie spoke about the importance of meals in their family ("always a big deal"). Friday night dinner in particular was important in this Jewish family: "There was always Shabbos (sabbath) dinner . . . at my grandparents' house until my grandma got too frail, then it moved over here [to my mother's house]." Judy spoke of those Friday night dinners as "sacred." "If the kids were going out, they were not allowed to go out until after dinner. . . . It might be late." When Natalie moved away from the city where her parents live, she didn't have Shabbos dinner, "because I didn't have a family." Later, she worked at a synagogue and had dinner there on Friday. Now she has Shabbos dinner with her sister Heidi's family, since they both reside in the same city.

The young narrator of the movie *Soul Food* comments on the importance of his grandmother's Sunday dinners for the extended family at her Chicago home: "Big Mama kept us together." In *All Our Kin*, her classic case study of African American life in a Midwestern city, Carol Stack writes of how, when the Jackson family's relatives come unexpectedly from St. Louis or Chicago, "it is the occasion for a big and festive meal. The women devote all day to preparing it." She goes on to describe a typical spread: fresh coconut for hors d'oeuvres, followed by a dinner of greens, egg pie, sweet potatoes, buttermilk biscuits, and chicken.

Women usually play a key role in organizing extended family dinners. Eighty percent of daughters surveyed consider their own mother's role in such events important, and 86 percent rate their mothers' contributions positively. Seventy-nine percent say other women's role is important as well. Lots of women, then, are busy preparing these meals for extended families. Their prominent role illustrates sociologist Alice Rossi's observation, based on her study of intergenerational relations, that "the mother-daughter relationship is pivotal to the structure of the . . . ties that hold families together. . . . *Women are the unsung heroines of social integration:* . . . women provide the glue that holds families and lineages together."

The older generation eventually ceases to carry on, prompting others to take up the challenge. One survey respondent in her thirties writes that her mother, after many years of cooking, no longer cared to cook, so her sister took over, having everyone to *her* home for meals—"to keep the family connected." The importance of meals in accomplishing family connections is evidenced by Kraft Kitchens' recent announcement of a contest to find "the top 365 ideas that moms have about how families can reconnect with food at mealtimes." *Mom* is defined for contest purposes not as biological mother, but as "whoever keeps the household running and the family members connected."

## MAJOR HOLIDAYS

Often our extended family gatherings occur at major holidays/ holy days—Thanksgiving, Fourth of July, Easter, Passover, and Christmas. The table is important. Again, we are reminded, "If an event is meant to matter emotionally, symbolically, or mystically, food will be close at hand to sanctify and bind it." And the food offers quite practical benefits. As with the nuclear family, meals taken with the extended family can help smooth troubled waters, or, at the very least, serve as a distraction. One food writer puts it this way:

Without food, plenty of it and lovingly prepared, we might kill one another. . . . Even if we can't agree on which of a dozen names to call God, which profession is honorable or how much money is enough, why Sally married such a ne'er-do-well . . . or if retiring to California made Mom and Dad ditsy, it is incumbent upon every member of the flock to admit that the grub was good, then join in the consensus that seconds are in order. A baked ham inspires truce. A turkey levels dissent. The emblem of harmony and goodwill is manifested in a leg of roast lamb. Indeed, a holiday meal opens a window into the true spirit of kin.

Seventy-three percent of survey respondents agree that the family is able to put aside divisions at a special family meal. The tendency is to set aside disagreements and hurts, apparently, until another time.

The food is usually abundant and often elaborate at holiday meals. My mother—always generous in her offerings at the table—really went all-out at Thanksgiving and Christmas. There would be relish trays, several salads and vegetables, two or three kinds of meat, two kinds of dressing for the turkey (with or without oysters, in our tradition), fruitcake and pie, and ambrosia (food for gods indeed). These lavish feasts must have been exhausting to prepare, but what memories they call forth! And it is true that we were able to put aside our differences to enjoy these celebrations. I envision my late brother, whose political hero of the day I typically regarded as public enemy number one, digging into the food on his plate, and, without looking up, commenting, "Nobody can cook like Mama." On this we could all agree: She was a great cook.

Some memoirist daughters paint vivid word pictures of their mothers' holiday meals. In writing of her own childhood Christmases, Lillian Smith recounts in detail the tastes, aromas, activities, and excitement of Christmas day in her family's North Georgia home in the early part of the twentieth century. Regarding her mother, she writes, "She was an artist in her own kitchen and there was a deep pleasure in her eyes as she gently pushed prying little ones away, and went on with her creating." In this case, her mother was creating fruitcake. But Smith describes in great detail the preparation of "succulent [turkey] dressing made of nuts and oysters and celery and eggs and bread and turkey 'essence,' " ambrosia, and other dishes for the dinner. "All of this was unforgettable, seeping not only into memory but into bones and glands." For many women, as for Smith, "The greedy memory of childhood holds it all."

Holidays bring members of the extended family together in the kitchen as well as at the table. Some women enjoy a special bond with their mothers-in-law in the kitchen during these times. In our interview, Jacqueline, whose own mother is no longer living, related her experience with her husband's mother: "Granny G has come for Thanksgiving almost every year for the last thirteen or fourteen years. . . . We're in the kitchen, and she's all excited about what size turkey I've got, and it reminds me of my mother. And Granny G does the gravy always. . . . There is much talk and chatter in the kitchen. . . . I look forward to that."

Jacqueline contributed to the book her own mother's recipes for Southern cornbread dressing and giblet gravy from their traditional family Thanksgiving menu, adding this comment: "My mother, Mrs. Ella Mae Webb, was the best mother and homemaker I've ever known." Jacqueline hails from the same part of Georgia as my mother, and the food is strongly reminiscent of the holiday food I know. (I nearly swooned when we talked about giblet gravy.)

# Southern Cornbread Giblet Dressing and Giblet Gravy
Jacqueline Richardson
Ella Mae Webb

## Dressing

For two quarts of dressing or enough for a 12- to 14-pound turkey:

6 cups crumbled corn bread (can use some regular bread crumbs or leftover grits, if desired)

turkey giblets and neck water

1 large onion, chopped

3 to 4 stalks of celery, chopped

2 cups turkey broth

1 or 2 eggs, lightly beaten

1 teaspoon salt

1 teaspoon poultry seasoning, or more, to taste

½ teaspoon sage

pepper to taste

Crumble the corn bread, breaking up into crumbs, or until texture is fine. Bring turkey giblets (liver, neck, etc.) to boil in water, with some salt and pepper sprinkled in water. Reduce heat and simmer about 15 minutes. Remove liver and continue cooking another 20 minutes or until giblets are tender. Remove giblets, cool slightly and chop coarsely. Reserve the neck and some of the giblets for giblet gravy (recipe below). Mix 1 to 2 cups chopped giblets into the corn bread.

Simmer the onion and celery in the turkey broth about 15 minutes or until vegetables are softened slightly. Pour broth and vegetables into the corn bread and giblets and stir in eggs, salt, poultry seasoning, sage, and pepper, if used. (If turkey broth is not fat, add a little melted butter to dressing for extra flavor and moistness.) Add more broth if needed to make moist dressing.

If the dressing is being prepared ahead, cover it tightly and refrigerate immediately. When ready to cook turkey, fill cavity lightly with dressing and secure opening with picks and clean string. Roast turkey immediately, following directions on turkey label. Cook any extra dressing in a lightly buttered, covered casserole dish by baking at 350 degrees 30 to 45 minutes or until dressing is heated through. Uncover casserole and continue to bake until top is lightly browned.

### Giblet gravy

For 2 to 3 cups of gravy:

½ cup fat from roasting turkey

¼ to ⅓ cup flour

1 cup chopped turkey giblets and meat from cooked turkey neck

2 to 3 cups turkey broth

salt and pepper to taste

Heat fat in a small skillet. Sprinkle in the flour, stirring and cooking until well blended. Slowly stir in the hot turkey broth, cooking and stirring until thickened slightly as desired for gravy. Add turkey giblets and neck meat, salt and pepper to taste, heat thoroughly and serve immediately with turkey and corn bread giblet dressing. (A chopped, hard-cooked egg can be added to this gravy. If more gravy is needed, add turkey broth and some of the dressing, which will thicken the gravy if stirred in and cooked into it.)

Grandmothers stand out in holiday kitchen memories of many women. A fifty-one-year-old registered nurse writes, "At Christmas, both my grandmothers would come to my mother's, and they would bake cookies all day long. That was a wonderful time! I still make four or five varieties of Christmas cookies using the same cookie cutters. It is a wonderful recollection and very satisfying for me, although I am usually doing it alone. When I use the cookie cutters, it feels like I am holding hands with my mother or my grandmothers."

Melissa, twenty-nine, told the *Minnesota Women's Press* of the wonderful memories of Thanksgiving and Christmas at her grandmother's house. The women of her family gathered in the kitchen to make Norwegian holiday treats such as rosettes and *krumkake*.

"The smells were incredible. And I loved how the conversation overlapped and circled around the kitchen." Her best memories of special events and holidays are of doing the dishes afterward with all the women in the kitchen talking, laughing, and telling stories. "It's when the real conversations happened."

Baked goods are a special feature of holiday cooking. Many mothers do a great deal of cookie baking at holidays, even now, when they are working outside the home. Broadcast journalist Cookie Roberts comments on her annoyance when she read an article in a local newspaper about how "a working mother wouldn't be able to bake with the children, hand down the cookie recipes from generation to generation." She thought of her cabinet full of various holiday cookie cutters and of all the hours she has spent making, and helping her children make, holiday cookies.

Jeanne C. spoke at one of the first focus groups about making Christmas cookies with her daughter. She then sent family recipes that her daughter especially likes. This one comes from Jeanne's mother.

## Nutmeg Sticks
Jeanne Cornish
Helen Morris Wright

Jeanne's note: I have no idea where my mother got this recipe, but it became a Christmas-time favorite. This past Christmas Eve, my youngest daughter Julie (now 28) and I set aside some time to do some Christmas baking. This was the first recipe Julie chose. As she was rolling the dough into "logs," she said she was making these in remembrance of her grandmother. They have always been one of her favorites.

### Cookie dough

Cream:

1 cup butter

2 teaspoons vanilla

2 teaspoons rum flavoring

¾ cup sugar

Add:

1 egg

Continue creaming mixture until well-blended.

Sift together, then add to creamed mixture:

3 cups flour

1 teaspoon nutmeg

¼ teaspoon salt

Shape into a roll (½- to 1-inch diameter) on a sugared cutting board. Cut into 2- to 3-inch-long pieces. Bake on ungreased cookie sheet 12 to 15 minutes at 350 degrees (cookies will still be white on top and just starting to turn light golden brown on the bottom). When cool, frost and sprinkle with nutmeg.

### Frosting

Cream:

⅓ cup butter

1 tablespoon cream

2 cups sifted powdered sugar

1 teaspoon vanilla

2 teaspoons rum flavoring

Beat until smooth. Add more powdered sugar if needed for spreading consistency. Spread on cookies as soon as the frosting is ready—before it starts to set up—so the nutmeg will stick.

The recipe makes enough for generous frosting of the nutmeg cookies with some left over to use on other cookies or to spread on graham crackers (which is what we always did when I was a kid when there was leftover frosting).

A family may have particular food items that epitomize a holiday for them. Often, these are baked goods. Pastor/writer Kristine Holmgren tells the story of how, in a year when the budget did not allow for such luxuries, her daughters nevertheless insisted she make *krumkake*. They dug money out of their piggy banks to buy the necessary butter and cream for this traditional Thanksgiving treat. In addition to being a reminder of how much *krumkake* means to her children, that Thanksgiving was an occasion for Holmgren to reminisce about the meticulous procedures her mother followed to make this delicacy and to keep the required iron in good condition: "The key is vigilance."

Traditional foods can be especially important in a family where the daily food is undistinguished or where the mother does not normally invite children into the kitchen. One Texas woman, whose mother showed no particular skill at, or interest in, ordinary cooking, writes of special memories of "traditional food at Christmas—stollen for Christmas breakfast and . . . Christmas cookies." A Wisconsin mother who did not normally allow her daughters in the kitchen reportedly "softened and was very inclusive during Christmas baking, the way I wished she was all the time. She'd not even worry if a few grains of sugar got on the floor." The daughter telling this story continues the family tradition of Christmas baking with her own daughters and her partner. No one enjoys it more than she, though. "Long after everyone has gone to bed, I'm still in the kitchen, decorating away, using the very same patterns I used as a kid, feeling very secure and happy."

Natalie pointed out in our interview with her mother Judy and her sister Miriam that "Passover—the most observed holiday in the Jewish calendar—is totally food-based." The women in this family work together in the kitchen primarily when they are preparing the Passover meal. "People put lots of energy into it," said Natalie. "It is all about the food." She described one of her best memories—a Passover Seder with her mother's entire extended family. "We ordered in (from a caterer), but there was all kinds of preparation. I remember doing it with [my aunt and cousin]. It was really the women putting that whole thing together. . . . It was positive." Natalie's sister Miriam remembers as special a feminist Seder she attended with her mother. Judy recounted how that Seder began "a number of years ago," starting out with just her peers, then expanding to include their daughters. "The food is always fabulous," according to Judy.

The feminist Seder that Judy is part of is reminiscent of the annual Passover Seder E. M. Broner describes in *The Telling*. Subtitled *The Story of a Group of Jewish Women Who Journey to Spirituality through Community and Ceremony*, the book describes the extraordinary experience of a group of women, including Bella Abzug, Gloria Steinem, Letty Cottin Pogrebin, Phyllis Chesler, Lilly Rivlin, and Grace Paley, who began gathering annually in 1975 "to reclaim their religion by making women's voices heard at the Passover table." These women call themselves Seder Mothers and Seder Sisters—and they bring their daughters and surrogate daughters to the Seder.

As Jewish cookbook writer Kay Pomerantz notes, Jews "certainly are a people who love to celebrate at the table." She writes of the work, then the satisfaction, of making special foods for special days and, ultimately, "delicious memories to savor." The work is worth it, she says. Truly. Everything I know about these celebrations—directly and vicariously—bears witness to their power.

## OTHER SPECIAL OCCASIONS

Though holidays serve as primary extended family gathering times for many families, other events may also serve that function. In some families, the extended family gathers in greatest numbers not at holidays, but at family reunions. These gatherings occur yearly for some families, sporadically for others. Usually, food figures prominently. The Smith family, spread across the North American continent, gathers yearly at Big Ridge on the Virginia–West Virginia border. The Big Ridge community the eight elder Smiths grew up in no longer exists, having lasted for only one generation. Fred Smith, a son of one of the eight, recalls reunions on Big Ridge with as many as one hundred people. Regarding the place of food in the reunion, he says flatly, "The reunion *is* a meal." People drift onto the mountain as they are able, to join the group, but everyone who is coming is there for the meal. A huge buffet, to which all contribute, is spread on long tables. Aunt Fran directs the kitchen. Women are in charge, and even men such as Fred, completely at home in the kitchen, take little part in laying out the dinner.

The meal Fred describes brings to mind country church homecomings I attended as a child. Like the Smith reunion, these were summer events; their memory conjures up women in thin summer dresses, hovering over long tables as they fuss with food brought by themselves and others. My connection of church homecomings to family reunions is apropos in the case of the Smith reunion, which coincides with a once-a-year church service the first Sunday in August at the old Antioch Christian Church.

Contrasting with the Smith reunion, with its fixed setting and long history, is the Ferguson reunion, movable and relatively recently established. For the past decade, the four Ferguson siblings and their progeny have gathered annually to renew their ties. The tradition began after the death of the elder Fergusons as a way to ensure that the family will continue to come together as it did formerly at the family home. Now, one family group chooses the reunion location—typically a resort in the Midwest, to insure the least amount of travel for the greatest number—and makes the arrangements. During the reunion period, concentrated in three or four days, but extending up to a week for those who can manage a longer stay, one of the families assumes responsibility for each evening meal. As with the Smith reunion, women take the lead in providing food. Food items having special meaning for the family often appear on the menu, especially dishes Mother Ferguson, a Virginian, might have cooked. After the death of James, one of the four siblings, a meal featured his favorite foods. Food stories are told and retold at these gatherings, and food-related games, such as watermelon-seed-spitting contests, make up part of the fun.

Reunions such as these provide an opportunity to gather with and enjoy more family members than are usually present at holidays. The setting often offers out-of-the-ordinary pleasures. Meals taken together form the centerpiece. But another type of family gathering is occasioned by less happy events. While I was writing this book, such an event occurred, neither anticipated nor relished. My brother died after a short but rapidly progressing illness. Though not sudden, his death was devastating. One of the most comforting things that happened during that period was a meal provided by his wife's sisters following his burial. Those present gathered in the country church's social hall for a simple spread prepared by these gracious women. The main dishes they chose—Brunswick stew and barbecue—were all the more meaningful to me because for the past few years, when I have visited my brother, we've gone out for barbecue. The last time we did so, he praised the restaurant's Brunswick stew. He would have relished his post-burial meal.

Except in the case of deaths of close family members, I do not recall such formal post-funeral meals from the first half of my life. In the past decade or so, however, I have attended an increasing number of funerals followed by meals, sometimes at a church, sometimes at a restaurant, sometimes at the home of a family member of the deceased. These meals seem to me a fine way to allow people to talk with one another, comfort one another, and remember the deceased. The food is sometimes provided by a restaurant or caterer, sometimes by groups within religious communities who devote themselves routinely to this service.

In some traditions, the meal occurs *before* the funeral. Pauline Danforth describes a wake in the Ojibwe tradition—in this particular case, the urban wake—and women's place in providing the food. Soon after arriving at the wake, Danforth, second cousin to the deceased, a seven-year-old child, gravitates to the kitchen with a cousin.

Since we aren't closely related [to the deceased] and are in our middling years, it is our unspoken role. The kitchen is already busy with other women mixing the dough for fry bread and accepting the many donations of food being brought in. My older cousin Mary, trained as a cook, moves efficiently here and there, working in tandem with her cousin Poncho, who . . . I decide is the "head cook"; she was here first and knows what's going on. She puts me to work at the industrial-sized metal table making bologna sandwiches and opening cans of tuna and peas for a tuna noodle casserole. My cousin Sue meanders in and is immediately given an apron and asked to fry bread. . . . It strikes me that my role and the roles of my same-age cousins have changed. We've all attended Catholic wakes since we were children living on the reservation. . . . Now we are the strong ones, caretakers of the children and elders. . . .

She continues her description of what happens in the kitchen— the women of her generation cooking and the children and others wandering in to "visit." Finally, the women serve the meal. A "spirit dish," containing a teaspoonful of all the dishes, is left for the departing spirit, and the food left reserved for "another round of feasting." For the Ojibwe wake, a mix of Catholic and Midewiwin religious traditions, will be repeated again on the reservation the day before a funeral mass is celebrated and the child subsequently buried in the Catholic cemetery.

When I interviewed Judy and her daughters, they talked about the Jewish practice of family friends providing food during shiva, the period of mourning observed in the home after the death of a family member. Shiva lasts traditionally for seven days. "The first thing you do after the funeral is come back to the home to have a meal. Friends take charge. It just 'happens.' " Judy described the "beautiful way" her friends provided food for this meal after her mother's death. "My friends were so fabulous. They just came in and did. They washed dishes, cleaned up the kitchen." The bringing of food continues throughout the seven days of "sitting shiva," a tangible way of saying "I'm sorry for your loss."

Such are the ways that food is featured in some of the special occasions families observe. When we remember these occasions, we often think in fact about the food, picturing the table in our mind's eye. As creatures, we must eat. But the food at these events offers far more than nourishment. Taking it with others offers a way to reconnect and catch up; to remember, celebrate, and mourn; to show we care.

## CHANGING MORES AROUND DINING IN FAMILIES

Given the centrality of meals in family life, their status calls for an accounting. Social changes of the last few decades have altered, and continue to alter, our habits. Some of those changes affect the family table. Patterns of dining and sex role shifts bear particular attention.

### Dining Patterns

It is common now to hear comments like "Families don't sit down to meals together anymore." Instead, it is said, everyone eats on the run, or individual family members eat on their own schedules, alone. This idea was voiced by a fourteen-year-old in one of the interviews: "I don't think eating is as enjoyable as it used to be when people sat around a table. . . . It doesn't happen around a table now. . . . People grab something. Some watch television while eating." A Kentucky psychiatrist, mother of two adult children, puzzles over their ways of eating: "They eat on the bed. ??????" In addition, we hear, people take their meals in restaurants, fast-food or otherwise.

Chuck Williams, founder of Williams-Sonoma, a purveyor of fine cookware and cooking supplies, notices the difference. "People are buying more [cooking paraphernalia] today than they bought before, but they are not cooking the way they used to; they are not cooking three meals a day." He goes on to say that home baking has decreased due to the time factor. Though many people bake bread, they use a breadmaker rather than baking the old way. On the other hand, "There's not much baking of cakes and pies at home anymore," according to Williams. Indeed, signs of this change are evident in more places than homes. A volunteer at my church told me recently that we are no longer able to get members to offer home-baked goods for our spring festival. Why? I asked. All the people who used to do that are "gone," said my friend. My church is not unusual; others, too, face the impossibility of carrying on as before, without the volunteer help of women now working outside the home.

There is, indeed, change in our dining patterns, but the change may not be so drastic as some commentators suggest. Poll results on in-home dining provide a reality check. A 1995 Roper poll reported "slightly more than half" of American families eat together five or more days a week, a decrease of about 18 percent in two decades. This corresponds roughly to my survey results, representing practices of several hundred homes around the country, in which 49 percent of women say their families have dinner together every day, or most days. Only 2 percent report never having dinner together.

These results suggest that, although regular in-family dining is decreasing, death notices for the family dinner implicit in such remarks as "People don't eat together anymore" are premature. Around half of American families have dinner together regularly, in fact. Historian John Gillis reminds us that "we tend to exaggerate the frequency with which families ate together in the past and to underestimate the commitment to the family dinner in the present."

As for the extent to which households eat out, 21 percent of survey respondents say they buy *no* dinners out in a week, and another 46 percent eat out once or less a week. Twenty-eight percent buy no takeout dinners (or parts of dinners) in a week, 43 percent do so up to once a week, and 20 percent do so once to twice a week. Women living in a household with others report buying an average of 1.2 meals out a week and purchasing all or part of meals as carryout an average of once a week. (The figures are greater, but not dramatically so, for women living alone.)

While there has been growth in the amount of dining out in the past few decades, household size and whether or not children are present affects how much dining out a family does. In families with children, not surprisingly, the younger the children, the less the family eats out. In a 1997 Gallup poll replicating one of fifty years earlier, over 70 percent of parents with children under eighteen say they have at least five of seven dinners a week as a family. Moreover, nearly two-thirds of those report saying grace out loud, up from 43 percent half a century before. The poll offered "no dramatic evidence . . . that today's families are so widely pulled apart by their various activities that they eat on the run." In the Harvard Medical School study cited earlier, 83 percent of children aged nine to fourteen years ate dinner with the family most days or every day. A recent survey of U.S. workers, in fact, reveals that working parents are spending *more* time with their children than was the case two decades ago. While these parents would like still more time with their children, the picture is improving, due primarily to changes in fathers' behavior.

Children's reactions underscore the impact of meals on their welfare. Research on the nation's children showed recently that frequency of meals with [at least] one parent correlates with positive feelings about parents' management of work and family responsibilities and other indicators of well-being, such as feeling important and loved.

While it is important to look at statistics that offer correctives to oversimplifications about frequency of family dining, many observers see, and have concerns about, those families with no commitment to common meals. During our discussion of the "in-

### "ONE BIG HAPPY" by Rick Detorie

violate" Friday dinner of her childhood home, Natalie, who works with families in Chicago, spoke of how uncommon such a commitment is. "I've worked with so many families, and I see them never having [common meals]. I see [the lack of] it in them. There's always this 'Everybody's too busy.' There has to come a point where you're not too busy."

We need to ask ourselves if something valuable is lost when families do not dine together regularly. Many women say this is the one time family members gather in a group and face one another. The table requires us to consider others, to pay attention to others' needs. It requires us to listen, and it gives us an opportunity to be heard. As Lynne Rossetto Kasper notes, "What's important is talking and looking across the table at each other." She points out that it is no accident that world summits are held around tables, "because the primary significance of a table is that ... that's where people come together." If the trend away from family meals taken together continues, what ways of coming together will replace them? A sobering question.

## Gender Role Shifts

Changes in patterns of meal provision result partly from the increase in women's participation in the workforce outside the home. Some children, for example, came home for lunch from neighborhood schools when more mothers worked primarily at home. Few children do so now, due partly to a change in school attendance patterns, including the shift from the neighborhood school model, but also because no one is at home, often, to be with the youngsters. A mother and daughter interviewed, however, remember having lunch together on schooldays. Anne W., who grew up in Massachusetts, remarked, "I came home to lunch! And Jenny did too!" Daughter Jenny, who grew up in Minnesota, remembers: "I had spaghetti. . . . Sometimes we had picnics on the lawn at lunch."

Closely related to women's work outside the home is men's increased involvement in meal provision. My spouse provides half the evening meals we consume, and that is the case with many couples we know. In some households, men prepare most of the meals; eight percent of survey respondents report this phenomenon in their living situation. During my interview with one mother-daughter pair, both of whose husbands cook, the mother remarked that she has always been involved with men who cook. Her current husband cooks most of the family meals, and her first husband, the father of her three children, cooked on weekends during their marriage. This woman's daughter remarked that, in spite of her father's cooking only this fraction of the meals, "Of course, Dad got to be the star. . . . Mom, the feminist Ph.D., still cooked five meals a week and Dad [was seen as] the hip, progressive dad."

But this reaction is not unusual. Men get a great deal of credit for the cooking they do. Accordingly, in Rose Glickman's *Daughters of Feminists*, a book based on interviews with the young women of the title, food comes up as a topic rarely, except with reference to *men* who cook. My survey results also reflect women's interest in such men. A twenty-seven-year-old public health educator reports her mother's very sound advice to "be involved with men who cook, or are willing to learn to cook." (Her mother married such a man.) Others note that their fathers carried the responsibility for cooking. After writing of the richness of her mother's contribution to her life through food, a forty-year-old Michigan woman relates her father's role in holiday meal preparation during her childhood and in the early years of her parents' marriage:

I . . . had a great time with my father for a number of years. I would incite him to great culinary feats at holidays: real plum pudding, beef

Wellington, lobster diablo, etc. Drove my mom nuts, too—because the kitchen was *her* turf, not Dad's! Ironically, when they married he did all the cooking—she couldn't cook—*her* man dominated their kitchen!

Men's involvement in cooking and other household chores has certainly increased since women added work outside the home to that inside the home, but, as noted earlier, women still carry the preponderance of that responsibility, according to studies of household labor, time studies of everyday life, and my own research. (See also discussion on cooking as "woman's duty" in Chapter 7, and associated notes.) And this is what the younger generation of women must contend with. Reorganization and reassignment of household work has in no way caught up with the pace of social change.

In most of the households I surveyed, someone is preparing meals. Most women value the provision of family meals, and they remember what their mothers did in their childhood homes. Current trends in restaurant dining may in fact *demonstrate* those memories of meals at home. One chef-teacher from the prestigious Culinary Institute of America remarks, ". . . Americans increasingly yearn for food that feeds the soul. One big trend over the past decade has been toward home-style cooking in restaurants." He notes that many American restaurants menus include or feature foods remembered from childhood. The desire appears to be present for home-cooked meals; their execution simply proves more difficult nowadays.

Many parents (and surrogate parents) still scramble to provide meals for the family; many feel inadequate and conflicted about the way they manage family meals. Columnist Marla Paul writes of uneasiness about her cooking practices in her modern household. Her husband works late, so the effort to cook for herself and her daughter seems overwhelming. She notices, though, that her daughter seems "nervous" about the "haphazard" dinner arrangements in their household. She vows to change her practices toward the "comfortable ritual" that dinner was in her own mother's household. Similarly, a working mother told researcher Arlie Russell Hochschild, ". . . I don't give my child as much as my mother gave me. That's why I want my husband involved—to make up for that."

Implicit in these women's concerns is their recognition of food's importance in the family. Social change notwithstanding, nothing has replaced the table as the primary place to come together as a household, or as an extended family. The act of dining together holds meaning beyond tradition. The family table's value as a setting to socialize and teach children remains important and, for that reason alone, its health is important to the common good. But the table is also where we know, and are known to, one another. A social institution, it requires attention for health and preservation, especially in a time when many have already pronounced it dead.

Women's responsibility for meals in the past, and, for the most part, in the present, means that mothers and daughters are linked through food in ways fathers and sons are not. Yet modern women's lives are vastly different from those of our grandmothers, unfolding in a vastly different landscape. That food is both fuel, which we must have, but more than fuel, a "symbol of joy and abundance in life—a way to cherish a place, a person, a moment in time," many of us do not question. As we look at some ways that food connects mothers and daughters—both in the settings described in this chapter and in others—we may find not only appreciation for the past but inspiration to help us negotiate the future.

# 3

# "The Best Thing": Communication about and through Food

When I was seventeen years old, I left home to attend college. I lived at home only a couple of summers after that, and during visits. When my mother and I did talk, usually by phone from afar, food was often a topic of conversation. I always listened with interest to what Mama had for dinner, since, when I lived alone, my miserable cooking skills did not make for memorable meals. When I began cooking more seriously, especially during the early years of marriage, pushed beyond my capacities by stepping into the traditional role of providing most of our evening meals, I asked her for recipes. Like so many accomplished cooks, my mother did not cook from recipes. (One woman goes so far as to assert that no "real cook" uses recipes.) Nevertheless, my mother told me what to do to make a given dish, and I wrote it down. Or, if there was time in between the asking and the need, she composed a recipe and sent it to me. It was in this way that I acquired recipes for such standbys as salmon croquettes, meatloaf, cornbread, spaghetti sauce, and coleslaw. Though I may change these recipes—I use oat bran instead of cracker crumbs in my salmon croquettes, for example, and serve them with salsa, a product unheard of in my childhood home—I still use them, and doing so makes me happy.

For Mama and me, food served as common ground, as it does

for many mother-daughter pairs. This is no small thing. As many of us, as adult daughters, become further and further removed from our roots—geographically, economically, and socially—whatever brings us together with our mothers has importance. A Virginia woman expresses it this way: "We both love food—eating it, talking about it, going to restaurants—so it provides an important link for us. We don't get along in other ways, but we always find common ground in food." Jeanne E. giggled, during an interview with her mother, as she said, "Mom likes to eat, you know. *We like to eat*." Three women in their 50s write about "the best thing about my relationship with my mother through food":

- It's a place (maybe the only place) in our relationship that is relatively balanced and stress-free. (Minnesota artist)
- After I married, that was the one thing that bridged the gap from teen years to adulthood to help us bond. (Texas photographer)
- My mother . . . has had great difficulty being nurturing and supportive, yet food is . . . a way we can communicate—safely and positively. (Pennsylvania nurse)

But younger women, too, find food to be common ground.

- [It's an] opportunity to talk about a wide variety of topics. (Minnesota educator)
- We both enjoy inventive cooking. (New York college student)
- We never argue, because we're eating. (Michigan college student)

The Michigan student's wry comment suggests, along with others, that some women find food provides relief in an otherwise contentious relationship. While my own relationship with my mother could not be termed contentious, we had our struggles, including some serious ones. Food was always a uniting experience and something stress-free to talk about.

Food, then, offers an occasion for, and a topic of, communication between mothers and daughters. This chapter shows how being together in the kitchen, or in other food-related settings, can facilitate communication, and how food figures in telephone conversations, letters, and other mediated exchanges between mother and daughter.

# DIRECT COMMUNICATION

## Conversation in the Family Kitchen

The kitchen, "the emotional center of the home," is the primary gathering place in many households. When I asked Ruth and her daughters, during our interview, if kitchen communication was common, hysterical laughter erupted. Ruth finally responded, "In our house, the kitchen is where *all* conversation happens." A forty-four-year-old survey respondent writes similarly of her mother's kitchen: "The kitchen is where everything happened. When we were at home we often were in the kitchen."

Inevitably, then, as a communication center for the entire household, the kitchen serves as the locus of communication between mother and daughter. Luce Giard calls kitchen time "the time of blessed intimacy," and it was certainly that for my mother and me. The men in my family at that time did *nothing* in the kitchen, except eat, so it was just the two of us. Weekdays, my mother came home from work after six o'clock and, after changing her clothes, headed straight for the kitchen to start dinner. Unless I had an "event," such as a choral performance, debate match, or early date that included dinner, I took my seat at the table beside the stove in our tiny kitchen. While Mama cooked dinner, a spread that often included homemade biscuits or cornbread, I told her about the events of my day. She listened while she worked, and she commented. She often told me, too, about what was going on in her life at work—some worry about an employee she supervised, a problem she needed to solve, a conversation she'd had with her boss.

While we talked, I usually set the table and occasionally gave her minor assistance, such as slicing tomatoes. After dinner, I dried the dishes while she washed, and we talked some more. It was during those times that she gave me encouragement to do my best—and tried to tone down the brashness I was capable of. After finishing the dishes, we moved on to our individual concerns—typically, for me, homework and telephone conversations with friends; for her, reading the paper and seeing to her work clothes for the next day.

Mama's life seems painfully constrained to me now as I look

back on it. And I am truly amazed that she was able not only to cook a full dinner after work, but to attend to me while doing it. She must have been very tired. This was the South of the forties and fifties. The weather was warm a good bit of the year, and really hot sometimes, and we had no air-conditioning. Even worse, Mama worked all day in an industrial cafeteria, also without air-conditioning, supervising the kitchen and steam table workers. From a modern perspective, her life focused more on toil than seems healthy. She had virtually no time to herself. But one thing I know she accomplished as she cooked dinner for us every night was paying attention to me and passing on values that have served me well—hard work, high standards, honesty, and caring.

Other women, too, value time spent with their mothers in the kitchen. They, too, enjoyed the good smells, the activity, and the conversation. A twenty-six-year-old accountant writes of her experience with her mother: "[Food] always brought us together. She opened up the most in the kitchen. She has an energy about her as she cooks. She is positive, and we are usually laughing the most in the kitchen. . . . In the kitchen is when we usually communicate the most." A California homemaker echoes the special openness of kitchen talk, pinpointing the best thing about her food relationship with her mother as "the way we are able to open up more freely to each other . . . in the kitchen."

Some women remember especially well their mother's kitchen during their childhood. They mention how their mothers provided treats for them and how much they looked forward to that and to conversation. Steph, twenty-two, told *Minnesota Women's Press* how, when she was in junior high, she and her mother shared a big bowl of popcorn and orange juice after school. "I'd tell my little junior high problems." She and her mother look back on that now as special time spent together. Women who worked at home all day when their children were growing up were able to be there for that kind of talk. Kathleen, a woman of my mother's generation, seized the opportunity. She found her children were "bubbling" when they came home from school, and she felt if she wasn't there to listen, she "wasn't going to hear about it." One daughter was the appointed baker in the family, supporting the after-school chats by providing home-baked cookies to go with the ritual cocoa. From the mother's point of view, as well as the child's, the after-school period could be the best time of the day. Such was the case with Judy, mother of three daughters, who remarked that her kitchen table "has seen lots of conversation."

A couple of mothers who went to work outside the home after their youngest child entered school knew the importance of time with children in the kitchen and accomplished that during preparation of the evening meal. Mary M. noted her conscious decision, when she resumed paid work outside the home, to make a point of cooking supper so that she'd be "in tune with the kids and know what was going on with them." Her older daughter Molly noted in their interview that the picnic table in their large kitchen was not only a good place to talk but the "ideal layout for homework, or for talking on the phone." Each child had a cubbyhole for personal belongings there as well, making it a more than usually inviting spot to roost.

In *Composing a Life*, a book examining the lives of five contemporary women, Mary Catherine Bateson weaves in food repeatedly, especially when writing of her own life and that of her late mother, anthropologist Margaret Mead. Bateson's household is no traditional one; her spouse shares the cooking, and, as a professional who often works at home, she struggles to "resist the temptation to chip away at my workday by spending extra time on food preparation." She writes, nevertheless, of the importance of the kitchen for a working mother "searching for quality time" with her daughter: "I have become convinced that the best times actually occur in the kitchen or the car, when some simple task like shelling peas or getting to the supermarket defines the time and space in which to build and strengthen our communication."

Many daughters agree with Bateson. A Michigan woman in her sixties writes, "The kitchen was a cheerful place, and [my mother] was happy while cooking or canning, and we talked. I studied there as I was growing up." The words of an Iowa county assessor show how special this common time together could be: "It was 'our time.' With four sisters and four brothers, time alone with Mom was precious. I was oldest and got home first. I worked on homework at the kitchen table, and we talked about everything while she cooked. I helped when I finished my homework." A Minnesota office manager was especially tuned in as a child to the sensory delights in the kitchen, even as she talked with her mother. She describes the best thing about her connection with her mother through food as "the times spent in conversation, while watching the process of preparing foods from beginning to end, with always a 'special treat' waiting when the food item was completely baked or cooked. For example, she made little loaves of bread—especially set apart from the normal large portion prepared—for each of us for our very own." Another woman, a Massachusetts administrator, writes similarly of the combination of conversation and baking, in particular "It always opened up a conversation opportunity. I always looked forward to Saturday mornings, when baking was done for the week—homemade donuts, bread, pies. It was great fun to participate with Mother and Grandmother, who lived with us."

One daughter mentioned, during an interview, doing her homework at the breakfast table in the family kitchen. She looked at her mother and said, "We talked about sex there." Mother was taken aback: "*Really???*" Apparently, these conversations, no matter how important, don't leave the same impression on both members of the pair!

Sometimes, inevitably, kitchen conversations between mother and adolescent daughter involve conflict. In "Connected to Mama's Spirit," Gloria Wade-Gayles writes of herself as a teenager in the projects, sitting in her mother's kitchen, pleading for the expensive paraphernalia associated with making a social debut. Her mother is making corn cakes, pouring boiling water into corn, lard, and salt. "When the consistency was right, she began rounding the wet meal with her strong hands, never looking up at me." As her mother questions her ("What will it do for you?"), Gloria emphasizes what an honor it is to be chosen to be a debutante. The two talk back and forth about the so-called honor, the daughter downplaying the cost and the mother emphasizing the illusion of benefits. All the while, Mama shapes and fries the corn cakes ("perfect circles"), their popping in the pan punctuating the clash of values. For Mama's philosophy was that of the Movement— "Keep your eyes on the prize. Move on"—and being a debutante was *no prize to her*. "She had a way of seeing around sharp corners, over high fences, beneath thick layers of confusion and uncertainty to the very center of truth and practicality. She had 'a single eye,' she would tell my sister and me . . . [and] that 'eye' was focused on [us], on our wholeness, our ability to stand tall in the light of our own suns." Wade-Gayles here uses the kitchen to symbolize her mother's firm grounding. It serves as a place to communicate deep caring and strongly held values; it provides stability amid the conflict of generations.

The talk that occurs in the kitchen while Mother is cooking—with or without a daughter's help—can be valuable. Indeed, 72 percent of survey respondents report talking often with their mother while they worked together in the kitchen or while Mother worked in the kitchen (70 percent), and two-thirds regard such talks as important. Cooking together serves to build the relationship in a special way for some mothers and daughters. In her study of adolescent girls and their mothers, Terri Apter found that "doing things in the kitchen" was one of the girls' favorite ways of being with their mothers. Here they confided in Mother and shared ideas. A twenty-four-year-old California woman, for example, recalls, "There were times when we were able to communicate, and it was always when we were in the kitchen. I found that very interesting and enjoyable. Cooking with her was perhaps the only time I had to speak to her."

But when some mothers do all the cooking themselves, with daughters joining them primarily to talk, kitchen time still offers rich benefits. The experience of a California college student and her sister sounds much like my own: "There was a lot of communication going on between my mother, sister, and me during the times my mother was cooking. Whether we were helping her or not, we would always talk about events of the day or activities we participated in at school." Another college student, this one from Virginia, suggests why daughters come into the kitchen during meal preparation: "She always has time to talk when cooking." Simply the mother's continuing presence in the kitchen draws daughters in who want to talk.

Women who have enjoyed this communion in the kitchen with their mothers earlier in life find as adults that coming together there during visits provides especially needed time to talk. Marjorie Myers Douglas, who lived on a farm at some distance from her city-based parents for seventeen years, writes of how when her parents came for Christmas, she and her mother were impatient to "get at the turkey" and "our longed-for chance to talk." Marvalene Hughes writes early in her discussion of the African

American household that, when she visits her mother, "she seldom spends time having long heart-to-heart talks unless I sit in the kitchen and join her in her cooking."

So, kitchen talk does not end when daughters leave their mothers' homes but continues in adulthood. A Minnesota woman in her forties values "the camaraderie when [Mother and I] are in the kitchen. The kitchen table is *still* the best place to sit and talk." Indeed, says this woman, "Anything can be discussed in a kitchen." A Texas contract administrator, also in her forties, shows just how central the kitchen can be as a place to talk with Mother throughout the lifespan: "Most of my childhood *and* adult conversations with my mother were in the kitchen."

## Nonverbal Communication in the Kitchen

Some communication between mothers and daughters in the kitchen is nonverbal. One three-generation group of women, for example, described how amazing it is that, when they are all in the kitchen together, they don't get in one another's way. This contrasts with their experience with men in the kitchen. Mystery writer Martha Grimes shows how, through nonverbal communication in the kitchen, mothers may express anger, as well as harmonious feelings, toward daughters. When the young narrator appears late for daily salad duty at the Hotel Paradise, where her mother furnishes the meals, she receives no verbal bawling out but "a knifelike look" from her mother, followed by a nonverbal "licking." Preparing pork chops for browning, "cutting bits of bone from a pork chop with the cleaver seemed to sluice off the anger she felt for me as it went *whack* through meat and bone, as if she were saying, '*This* chop showed up—' WHACK!—'when it was *supposed* to—' WHACK!—'because this chop is *dependable*—' WHACK!"

The kitchen environment itself can communicate to daughters the state of the mother's health, both physical and mental. The French writer Colette relates how the physical condition of the kitchen indicated her mother's impending death: "It was not until one morning when I found the kitchen unwarmed and the blue enamel saucepan hanging on the wall, that I felt my mother's end to be near. Her illness knew many respites, during which the fire flared up again on the hearth, and the smell of fresh bread and melting chocolate stole under the door together with the cat's impatient paw."

My husband and I learned the truth of Colette's insight as we watched the decline of both our mothers. My mother-in-law's kitchen offered the best clues to how seriously her capacity to manage had diminished. A woman who had truly awed me with her perfect pastries and who faithfully prepared, and cleaned up after, three meals a day for more than six decades, she began to leave frozen meat on the counter for days, then refreeze it. Preparing a meal for herself and her partner of sixty-three years became next to impossible. The chaos of the kitchen mirrored the chaos wrought in their lives by age and illness. Based on the message from Mom's kitchen, and fearing for their safety, we helped them move to a residential community where they could have meals prepared for them and receive other assistance as well.

In my own mother's case, as her disability from disease advanced, the kitchen showed departures from her usual practice. Her meal preparation took more shortcuts. Her kitchen appliances revealed less-than-scrupulous cleaning. The garden having been grassed over, she cooked, froze, and pickled few summer garden fruits and vegetables. Her appetite disappeared, along with her zest for life. Clearly, things were not going well, and I noticed these signs on visits leading up to her death.

When I asked one mother-daughter pair about nonverbal signs of Mother's state in the kitchen, the daughter remarked that not *whether* her mother cooks but how she goes *about* cooking is more of an indication of her state. She noted that her mother—an eighty-four-year-old—is in the kitchen a great deal and that, in fact, she couldn't remember the kitchen *ever* being unused. Addressing her mother, she said, "Your state of mind is very evident by the way you are cooking. When you feel stressed out, it's quite evident by the way pots get banged around."

Daughters mention both time and money as factors creating stress for their mothers, for example, and show how they reveal this in the kitchen. A Michigan massage therapist describes her own mother's "frustration around always having to have a meal ready at 6:15 for seven people without much money." A Nebraska human services worker suggests two problems associated with lack of time to prepare food: "We'd often be rushed—things wouldn't turn out right, maybe burn." Interestingly, this same woman, now thirty-eight, notes that as a child she did not think of her mother as being a good cook, but that as an adult she views her mother's cooking as "fantastic." Perhaps experience and reflection have engendered a certain respect for the task her mother faced in her particular circumstances.

In addition to pressures such as time and money, daughters "read" other states from their mothers' demeanor. Some pick up on unhappiness and depression. A fifty-six-year-old educator describes her mother's case: "She was often unhappy. This was reflected in the time we spent together in the kitchen and elsewhere." A thirty-five-year-old aquatics instructor writes simply, "She was sad when she cooked." Cooking can be a healing activity, though, for some women, and that too is evident to their daughters in the kitchen. Judy, a writer-editor and former co-worker, told me a few years ago that her sister took her own life. Following that tragedy, Judy visited her mother regularly. After one such visit, she wrote to me, "This has been a really tough summer for my mother, [but] she was so much better this weekend . . . very busy canning tomatoes, freezing beans, making jelly. Just doing these things is very satisfying and healing for her."

The kitchen serves as a center for communication, then, both verbal and nonverbal, both joyful and painful. Whether the daughter works with her mother, or simply joins her there to talk, kitchen time offers the two an unmatched opportunity for connecting and learning what is happening in each other's lives.

### Eating Out

The home kitchen is not the only setting where food provides a context for face-to-face communication between mothers and daughters. Many dine out together. The pace of modern life has made dining out necessary at times. And, at least in families like my own, increased means to buy restaurants meals makes doing so easier. Not having to prepare meals and clean up afterwards, if that is their normal practice, frees mothers and daughters to engage in conversation without distraction. Over three-quarters of women completing the survey report eating out with their mothers.

Some women mention especially eating out with their mothers

as children. One forty-two-year-old who grew up in New York notes that her memories of food and her mother focus "not so much . . . on cooking at home but on eating out. I have wonderful memories of going out to lunch as a child just with my mother. I now very much enjoy taking just one of my two kids out for a meal. The kids' and adults' worlds were quite separate when I was a kid, so going out with my mother was a treat." The specialness of the simplest excursion with Mother is captured in a "Sally Forth" cartoon. Sally and her daughter Hillary have an ice cream cone while sitting on a park bench. "What do you like best, the ice cream or the cone?" asks Hillary. "The company," replies Sally. In the final frame, Hillary looks at her mother and says, "This is one of those 'Preserve the Memory Moments,' isn't it?" "The effortless ones usually are," is her mother's response. The five frames in between these two brief exchanges show just how effortless the occasion is. They simply sit on the beach without speaking, enjoying their ice cream cones together.

Some of my fondest memories of times with my mother during my childhood are of meals we had together in a downtown Atlanta cafeteria, usually connected with a shopping trip or doctor's appointment, but sometimes just for fun. Now, when I am on Peachtree Street in the heart of the hotel district, nostalgia takes over, and I think of lunches at the S&W Cafeteria, long since gone. No "chain" cafeteria (the only kind I ever see nowadays) even comes close to the S&W of my memory; or is it the retrospective of the child I was—the delight of having my mother's attention all to myself while enjoying good food with her—that makes the setting so incomparable?

Memories of the food enjoyed by young daughters on these excursions can be so vivid that, as adults, they can recall quite specific details. A forty-seven-year-old poet-teacher still remembers her favorite treats from the Pittsburgh restaurants and cafeterias of her childhood: "My mother was a 'working woman' and I was an only child. My father traveled . . . Tuesday-Thursday nights. Every Tuesday, [Mother and I] ate out—the Y Cafeteria (great vegetable soup) or Henderson's (great navy bean soup). Or, as I got older, I could take the bus and meet her for lunch in Horne's tearoom (pink lemonade) or a downtown cafeteria (prune whip), or Stouffer's (mulligatawny). Downtown meant 'fancy,' 'sophisticated,' two 'girls' out together." This woman remembers these excursions as her best connection with her mother through food.

For adult daughters living on their own, a meal with Mother in a restaurant can be an especially good way to connect. Both mother and daughter value the companionship, the privacy they enjoy without other family members around, and the special treats they enjoy together. One mother-daughter pair related that they plan a dinner out every couple of months. No one else is allowed, just the two of them. They look for restaurants that serve food they both enjoy but don't have at home—liver and sweetbreads, notably. Some mothers and daughters, on the other hand, have special places they return to repeatedly, such as a particular ice cream parlor. One pair told me that, wherever they go, they routinely share food from their plates, "even though we know it's bad manners." Since we had this conversation over dinner, I can attest that they do!

A thirty-four-year-old Virginian, whose mother rarely cooks, "now that all of us have left home," enjoys having a special connection with her mother while eating out. "Often our conversations begin or end with restaurant reviews. When we get together, we eat out almost every meal (including breakfast). At those times I feel very close to her." A Minnesotan of the same age finds dining with her mother equally conducive to intimacy: "Presently, I find we have the nicest conversation in restaurants while we are eating."

The positive experience of eating out with her mother carries over into a fifty-six-year-old Georgian's present relationships with other women. She writes of her mother, "She taught me the joy of lunch with ladies. She always made our shopping trips a time to have a special lunch out, one with a nice atmosphere and nice conversation. I have wonderful memories of those times with her. Not so much the food, but the time and conversations and the lovely environments. It has made me enjoy the same as an adult with friends, my daughters, and other young women."

Though food consumed on these outings may not be as important for some women as the time with Mother, for others, food is of more than passing interest. A daughter who particularly enjoyed dining out with her mother reports the special effort her mother made to obtain recipes for the daughter's favorite dishes from the restaurants they frequented. Another mother rises to the culinary challenge of reproducing the meals. These feats are recounted by her daughter, a twenty-seven-year-old clerk typist: "When I go to visit my mother, we always try a new restaurant, and we try to figure out how they make the food we ordered. The next time I visit her, she will have figured out how to make it, and she fixes it for me, then gives me the recipe."

My interview with the Hadfield-Fuller women followed close on the heels of Marlyn and her elder daughter Lynn's trip to Marlyn's ancestral Norway. The two spent weeks eating out every meal. They spoke in some detail of the food they enjoyed together. Lynn revealed their mutual love of food—and the bond that it is for them—when she related that on the Norway trip they each wrote down all the food they were served.

Dining out as mother and daughter provides an opportunity to practice what anthropologists Farb and Armelagos assert is the primary way of maintaining relationships in all societies—eating together.

## MEDIATED COMMUNICATION

### Telephone

In her book *We Are Our Mothers' Daughters*, journalist Cokie Roberts cites a poll showing that nearly all adult daughters talk with their mothers "at least once a week" and "nearly half speak almost every day." Most of this talk is done by phone. Roberts talks with her own daughter by telephone "all the time." Recipes are among the topics. Her book is laced with examples of the ways food links women in her family.

In *Eating Chinese Food Naked*, a novel in which food figures heavily, Mei Ng illustrates the ways food serves as a topic when mother and daughter speak by phone. Ruby calls and asks her mother, "Where were you yesterday?" Her mother, Bell, replies, "Look like a nice day, so I take a walk. I go up to the fruit store. The grapes look nice and big, so I buy a pound." The conversation continues through Bell's continued ramble in a nearby neighborhood: "They open up a new hamburger joint over there. You know me, I don't eat hamburger, but I go in and order a cup of tea. Seventy cents for a little cup of tea!" Later she admits she bought a fishburger; still later, she asks her daughter, "You eat yet? You better go get something to eat." Their conversation ends with a discussion about Ruby's estranged boyfriend. Ruby comments, "He's a grown man and he doesn't know how to eat. He takes all the good parts for himself." Her mother thinks, "Not knowing how to eat was worse than going with another woman." She ends the conversation with "I better go cook now." There's a great deal going on between Ruby and Bell in this novel, but food provides a common topic for them. And the connection does not end when the phone is hung up. "Ruby put the phone down quietly and pictured her mother in her . . . kitchen. . . . She imagined her mother rushing over to the rice barrel and measuring out a cupful. Then she would take the cleaver from the drawer and chop and chop." Later, Bell leaves her "recipe" for sea bass on Ruby's answering machine. Directions are loose, as mothers' recipes often are: "Pour a little soy sauce on it, not too much. Then steam it until it's done, maybe 20 minutes."

In a conversation about this book with my Chinese-American optometrist, she volunteered that any time she talks with her mother by telephone, the first thing her mother says is "Have you eaten?" I told her about *Eating Chinese Food Naked* and about food historian Yong Chen's comment that in some cultures food is as important as religion. "Absolutely," replied the doctor.

I asked the women I surveyed how many telephone conversations they had in a year with their mothers. They reported an average of 122 telephone conversations per year, with a high of 1825 conversations (one woman reports calling her mother five times a day!). Food plays a role in many of these conversations and sometimes serves as the main topic. My conversation with the Fuller-Hadfield women demonstrates why. Lisa, a thirty-six-year-old, addressed her mother in our interview, "When I think to tell you [by phone] about food, it's because I know you have an appreciation for good food. Or I think of you when I go somewhere. I think, 'Oh, Mom would love this.'" Her mother, Marlyn, commented on how food talk serves as a telephone conversation opener. "When we have houseguests, and Lisa calls, she says, 'I suppose you made them Norwegian pancakes!'" Her sister Lynn says she might ask, "What are you cooking?" She added, "I call my mom a lot when I'm cooking and don't know what to do."

# "Norweegies"
## Marlyn Hadfield

Marlyn's note: Some people call these Norwegian pancakes, but not me. For 3 to 4 servings, use:

6 eggs, beaten

1 cup milk

¾ cup flour

2 tablespoons sugar

¼ cup melted butter

¼ to ½ teaspoon cinnamon

Add to beaten eggs milk, flour, sugar, butter, and cinnamon, continuing to beat. Test batter on a hot griddle to be sure it's ready. Spread the batter with the back of the spoon. Pancakes should be very thin and nearly plate size. If you need to, for good consistency, add more flour or milk.

Serve with sour cream, fresh berries, jam, maple syrup, or whatever you like. After putting on topping choices, roll up and cut off a bite at a time.

"Whatcha got good to eat?" is another question frequently asked in telephone conversations, according to Elizabeth R., a daughter interviewed with her mother Mary G. Or, at Easter, Elizabeth might ask, "When are you making bunnies?" Mary carries on a family tradition of making bread in the shape of rabbits each year.

Obtaining recipes and methods of food preparation is one motivation for telephone calls for some women interviewed. Carol, a mother whose children have lived in distant cities, says she receives calls at least once a week for food help: "How do you do this? How do you do that? It's a big bond." Sometimes women's need for advice is urgent when they call their mothers. Often this occurs during holiday meal preparation, especially during the early years of living independently. Kevlyn said, "I can remember calling my mother in the middle of making gravy for Thanksgiving dinner, saying, *'This isn't working, Mother.'*" Anne W., a Massachusetts native, remembered in our interview, "My first Christmas in Minnesota, I had to call my mother about something like baked potatoes—too simple to be in a cookbook!" Anne's daughter Jenny recalls that, when she was in college in England for three years, she too telephoned her mother with food questions. Obviously, getting help on recipes can extend both throughout the family and across continents. Anne C., a woman whose immediate and extended family members live and travel widely, noted in our interview, "When I'm at home, I'm fielding recipe calls—from Iceland, France, Florida, California, the Czech Republic."

In her study of young adult daughters and their mothers, sociologist Lucy Rose Fischer found that the single most common kind of advice sought or received by married daughters related to cooking. Fischer found that "four-fifths of the married daughters . . . had asked for advice on 'how to cook a particular dish.'" (Seventy percent of my survey respondents report that their mothers contributed to their learning by answering their questions about cooking.) Daughters interviewed confirmed that they telephone their mothers with questions about cooking, and two-thirds of women completing the survey ask questions of their mothers about food at least sometimes. As daughters age, they are able in turn to offer their mothers help. One California woman in her forties writes of frequent calls to her mother in college and in the early years of marriage to get recipes. "Even now, when I can't find one, I call. She even calls *me* when she can't find *hers!*"

Sometimes it is the grandmother who receives the phone call about recipes, and daughters have particularly amusing stories about their grandmothers' instructions. Grandmothers seem even less likely than mothers to cook from recipes. Jeanne E. remembered in her interview, "As I started to cook more and more in my own household, I would call . . . Mom for specific recipes, or Grandma, when she was still alive. I can remember some very funny conversations with [Grandma]. One time was over the apple jelly: I remember cooking it, and I didn't know when to stop cooking it, but I did know that if I didn't stop soon enough it would be glue. So I called her, and . . . (I wish I had a recording of it) . . . she said, 'Well, all you have to do is look at the bubbles.' 'What am I looking for?' 'Well, when the bubbles come up and put a little ring around the pan, then you want to stick the wooden spoon in, and you want to look at the spoon.' " And so on. Eventually, this granddaughter got the information she needed.

Interestingly, food provides not only a topic of conversation between mother and daughter speaking by telephone; its use as a topic can even provide a means to achieve privacy. One woman reports that the only time she is able to talk with her mother by phone without her father on the line is when she and her mother turn the conversation to food: Her father hangs up at that point!

## Letters

Recently, looking in my files for a particular recipe, I found a scrap of a letter from my mother, written probably twenty years ago. "I'm going to make a green and gold squash casserole for dinner tonight," she began, then wrote out the recipe for me in her loopy script. She noted that the casserole could be used as a "meat substitute" and explained why. Her letter was written on both sides of the paper. On the other side was her plan to ask my brother, who lived in the area, to help her weed the cucumbers in her garden. She noted that every year she gave him pickles made from the various vegetables she grew or bought from her "produce man."

Apparently, other women have this kind of correspondence from their mothers as well. One woman who completed the survey returned it with a recent letter from her mother that she thought would be of interest. Two-thirds of the two-page letter dealt with food: menus for that day's and the next day's meals; plans for buying, processing and "putting up" midsummer produce; kitchen tool purchases she had recently made to render cooking and baking easier with diminished hand and arm strength; and a report on an extended family meal at a restaurant, in which she reported each diner's choice from the menu.

Perhaps the most extraordinary story of food as a topic in written correspondence, though, comes from Elizabeth S., a woman in her seventies who participated in one of my early focus groups. She and her mother wrote to each other weekly for forty-five years. Elizabeth reports never receiving a letter from her mother that did not include either a recipe or a menu. Often attendance at a luncheon or tea prompted the sending of these details.

A majority of women surveyed who do not live with or near their mothers write them at least one letter a year. The average number of letters written by these women per year is fourteen. As Ann Caron notes in her study of young women and their mothers, electronic mail (e-mail) has replaced letter writing for many young women. Some mother-daughter pairs use e-mail—daily, in some cases—to keep in touch. Seven percent of respondents to my survey use e-mail for correspondence with their mothers. Twenty-eight percent of letter and e-mail writers report that food is a topic in their correspondence.

A Michigan artist-writer-teacher writes about how her mother's focus on food forms the basis for their interaction: "Our correspondence/communication continues to revolve around food discussions . . . heavily intertwined with all the processing of food: shopping, putting by, dining out. . . . Today she's freezing cob corn for Thanksgiving dinner four months hence." But when food overtakes all else, women can tire of their mothers' preoccupation with food. One fifty-year-old New Jersey woman for example, wrote of the worst thing about her food connection with her mother: "As she got older, that was all she talked about. She was always asking me what I had eaten and what I was going to eat. However, it was only a lack of something to talk about. When she was younger, we never centered our conversations around food." Common ground may become the *only* ground for mothers who believe they have few other shared interests with their daughters.

The foregoing examples show how letters reflect women's food connection for the women contributing directly to my research. Looking into correspondence of women more broadly proves somewhat difficult, due in part to the relative scarcity of published and archived letters between mothers and daughters. Sadly, it is difficult to find even letters of famous women to their mothers. In developing a book of letters to their mothers by celebrated writers, Reid Sherline found "[t]he mother is as a general rule, absent, or nearly so, from published correspondence. Where letters are selected, the mother rarely makes the cut." According to Sherline, for example, the writer Colette wrote her mother more than 2000 letters; all were destroyed.

But a sample of letters between mothers and daughters that

Karen Payne has searched out (many of them unpublished) offers examples of how food figures in correspondence. In one, Isa Kogon writes to two of her three daughters about their lives. "Basically, I felt good about what both of you girls are doing. . . . The fact that all of you can cook a meal and stoke a stove doesn't go unnoticed either. I feel much pride in your homemaking skills, for your home is where your heart is, and there's much warmth in your homes." She ends her letter with "I feel a special gratitude that you chose me to be your mother. And on that note, I shall go cook a chicken and cluck some."

Sociologist Jessie Bernard's letter to her daughter, twelve weeks before her projected delivery, shows how she has worked to give her daughter strong nutrition *in utero*: "And how I have labored at that! I have eaten vitamins and minerals instead of food. Gallons of milk, pounds of lettuce, dozens of eggs . . . to make your body a strong one because everything [depends] on that. I would give you resiliency of body so that all the blows and buffets of this world would leave you still unbeaten." After her daughter's birth, she writes of her sadness that she does not have enough milk to nurse her.

### Visual Media

Women may use visual media as well in communicating about food. Though I posed no questions either in interviews or in surveys about visual media, examples of the use of film and video came forward. Beverly remarked during our interview, "There is no bigger central theme in my mother's life than food, and she passed that on to me." She followed up with examples of how the family uses photographs and videotapes to record food "events" and report them, especially to "Grandma Esther," her mother. They sometimes take photos of an especially nicely laid table, calling them "granny shots." Beverly had recently made a gift to her mother of a videotape of a trip some members of the family took to New England—"all food shots." Her mother was enthralled.

Apparently, photographing the table is not peculiar to Beverly's family. A freelance illustrator from Michigan writes in her survey that, in her family, "it is traditional to photograph the Thanksgiving table, sans people!"

Listening to and reading the ways women contributing to this book view food as a communication link between mother and daughter confirmed for me that my own experience was not unusual. The most common response, by far, to the open question, "The best thing about my relationship with my mother through food is/was . . . ," is the conversation and companionship enjoyed. Like me, many daughters find food serves as a focal point for being with their mothers. Even when their lives are far removed from one another's, food can play a role in bridging whatever gaps exist. For both those women and women with lives more similar in circumstances, it offers topics of conversation, a reason to get together, and an occasion for pleasure.

# 4

## "Secrets of Life": Food-Related Learning

James Boswell wrote in 1773 that he had found "a perfect definition of human nature": the human being "is a cooking animal." "No beast is a cook," according to Boswell. Nearly two and a half centuries later, science writer Susan Allport elaborates and updates: "We are the only animals to boil dry, bake, microwave, soak, and otherwise process plants to enhance their edibility.... there is something very powerful and fundamentally human about the transformation of raw food into cooked food." And, since it is overwhelmingly women who perform household cooking tasks across cultures, it is we who do the cooking that defines us thus.

Sixty-one percent of the women I surveyed cook, or prepare *something* to eat, *every day*. Only four percent never cook. Women who cook know something, at least, about what is involved in providing meals for themselves, if not for others as well. There are many aspects of food provision besides cooking proper, of course. Some of the communication between mother and daughters described in Chapter 3, involves learning—explicitly and implicitly—about acquiring, preparing, serving, and eating food. How women learn what they know about food, and how the mother-daughter connection contributes to that learning, is the subject of this chapter.

## LEARNING ABOUT FOOD FROM MOTHER

By contrast with their predecessors and with some women around the world, most modern American women are not systematically trained to prepare the cultural food. Historians Julia Cherry Spruill and Carroll Smith-Rosenberg describe how eighteenth-century and Victorian American women received careful training, from mothers who lived domestically centered lives, in the skills involved. But that has not been the case for some time, apparently. An example from my own youth demonstrates how it is that daughters of the twentieth century learned from Mother without being taught.

My mother made beautiful Southern biscuits regularly. I sat in the kitchen talking with her as she spooned what seemed to be a random amount of self-rising flour into a special bowl, scooped a piece of fat from a can and placed it in the center of the flour, poured in buttermilk, and worked the mass with her fingers. When the dough was "right," I watched her shape the biscuits, then place them on a greased baking sheet, blackened from many years' use. I could make those biscuits today easily, though Mama never taught me formally. Being in the presence of my mother, talking with her as she made biscuits, "taught" me.

Looking at ways women talk and write about how they learned about food and its preparation, I conclude that what most American women know about food happens informally, rather than through explicit teaching. As with young children's acquisition of language, exposure to food preparation and service ensures at least a measure of learning. Only one woman of the thirty-two I interviewed reports that her mother trained her "conscientiously" (her word). "It was what she thought she had to do. She always said that if she'd had a career, she'd have been a dietitian." (My own mother *was* a dietician, and, perhaps for that reason, did not have the *time* to train me!) Of women surveyed, only 16 percent report "comprehensive" training in cooking. Most report learning in a variety of ways, such as by being in the kitchen while their mothers cooked (79 percent), by watching (67 percent), and by learning from their mothers how to cook certain things (52 percent).

So this is the way many women learn—by being in the kitchen.

From the earliest years, daughters are present with Mother in the kitchen. The delights of the kitchen environment alone—aromas, camaraderie, energy—encourage learning. Luce Giard suggests a kind of "sensory and motor apprenticeship" children undertake in the kitchen: "The child looks, observing the mother's movements, admiring the strength of kneading hands; . . . learns to accomplish simple tasks (cracking open nuts without smashing them, pitting apricots, peeling apples); . . . learns the names of dishes and utensils, to differentiate action verbs or degrees of doneness." This sensory apprenticeship, hardly a training course in cooking, nevertheless sets the stage for learning about food preparation.

Kate L. described in our interview how she learned by being in the kitchen. "I feel like I've been cooking since I was five. I remember playing with pans and raisins and Cheerios and stirring. I definitely got the powerful feeling of cooking. . . . Just being in the presence of cooking is how you really learn." Women surveyed had similar experience. "[The best thing was] watching her. . . . She knew how to make anything and wasn't afraid to try something new or experiment. She always wanted me to help and learn how to cook; she was always willing to teach me," writes a twenty-two-year-old Illinois woman. A fifty-six-year-old Tennessee woman remembers watching as well: "I loved watching and seeing how everything went together just right and especially enjoyed the savory smells and flavors."

Some mothers set a stage that encourages their daughters to be in the kitchen. A twenty-one-year-old Californian describes her mother's way of influencing her, noting that being with her mother in the kitchen was "a fun experience. She never made me go into the kitchen with her but gave me sort of an invitation" and "didn't get mad if I didn't accept it."

Daughters present with their mothers in the kitchen may show curiosity about what is being done with food. But precise answers to questions are not always forthcoming. Peggy told the *Minnesota Women's Press* about being in the kitchen when her mother made egg noodles. "I remember how she made the well in the flour, how she kneaded the dough with her hands." When asked "how she knew how much flour to put in," Peggy's mother said, "You just know from the way it feels." I suspect that's where my mother would have started if I'd asked her how she knew when to stop "working" her biscuits and start shaping them for baking.

Carol, a woman in her seventh decade, describes her emotional response to memories of being with Mother in the kitchen as a youngster:

[When you told me about your project] . . . the most wonderful memories fluttered into my mind from my own childhood. My bond with my mother was so strong, and . . . it was forged in the kitchen. . . . She gradually let me take on roles. . . . I had never thought about how deeply I had anticipated [this], how important it was to me. . . . I wanted to be wherever she was. . . . Think where our parents were [in those days]; my mother was in the kitchen.

Taking on roles, as Carol puts it, enables daughters to learn how to do things with food. In *Miriam's Kitchen*, Elizabeth Ehrlich honors her mother-in-law, a woman who inspired a dramatic shift in her daughter-in-law's life. Miriam, "a keeper of rituals and recipes, and of stories," is asked by her granddaughter about how her great-grandmother and four sisters learned to cook.

"She taught them?" asks my daughter, innocent, sidling up to the counter, Barbie doll in hand.
"They helped her!" exclaims Miriam, with surprising vehemence.
[Ehrlich reflects:] For a moment I question the fashion in which I am raising my kids. I should be cooking and cleaning, my children beside me, so they also can learn the ingredients of everyday life.
"How else would she manage with nine children?"

Two-thirds of women surveyed report working with their mothers in the kitchen, and the same proportion report their work together went smoothly. Doing so helped them learn. Kevlyn spoke in our interview of how helping her mother gave her cooking skills as a girl: "I was lucky. When [Mother] was entertaining, especially, I helped, even at a very young age. I really believe that, by the time I was Sarah's [her fourteen-year-old daughter's] age, I could've put on an appetizer-type party." In another interview, Lynn, a forty-four-year-old, echoed this, remarking to her mother, "Hors d'oeuvres are my favorite thing to make and eat, and I think that comes from . . . help[ing] a lot when you entertained. Because we had back stairs in our house, we got to eat leftovers without having to meet the guests!" Like these women, Marilyn Stillman learned from helping. She views as her mother's "best gift" to her the opportunity to help in the kitchen as a girl.

Casey, who lived on a farm with her large family during hard times, remembers cooking meals when she was eight years old. "I loved it." Casey later trained and worked as a chef. Elizabeth S. remembers that Thursday night was the maid's night out. "So we would cook. I remember the first thing I ever learned to cook: an open-faced cheese, tomato and bacon sandwich." Jeanne E. noted that all her siblings had assigned jobs for meal preparation. Addressing her mother during our interview, she said, "I don't remember learning any particular dish from you, but I do remember being in the kitchen all the time and . . . doing hands-on kinds of things." And Jeanne's own daughters hang around when she's working in the kitchen—especially when she's baking. "Both of them like to poke in bread. They like to knead it. They like to steal it. They like raw bread dough. . . . Both of them take an interest when I'm baking."

Sixty-three percent of respondents believe themselves to be competent cooks, a belief that correlates with having asked Mother's help, having learned from watching Mother in the kitchen, having been trained by Mother, and having learned to cook certain things from Mother. Preparing a meal involves more than cooking individual dishes, however. Mother, as "repository for foodlore," in the words of anthropologist Eleanor Bauwens, imparts such knowledge as what goes with what, what tastes good, and what is good for us.

Planning a menu is one skill that daughters learn is important from their mothers. Mary Catherine Bateson's mother, Margaret Mead, had a standard menu for entertaining: steak, asparagus, and potatoes. Her advice to her daughter was to find similar ways to simplify entertaining. She suggested keeping a pot of soup simmering on the stove as "the symbol of loving effort without the hassle." Bateson did not follow in her mother's footsteps as a cook but prepared more elaborate meals.

An essential part of planning menus involves knowledge of nutrition. Some women write about learning to think in terms of balanced meals, to use fresh vegetables grown in the garden, and to avoid "junk food." Thirty-five-year-old Molly looks at a possible menu now and critiques it with nutrition in mind: "There's no green vegetable here." She says she learned this from her mother.

Other kinds of learning that women remember include table service, often taught by chores such as setting the table and getting the food on it. Pouring milk into a milk pitcher was a reminder, for example, that "you do not put cartons on the table," setting the table a reminder that "you always set a full place." A pair of daughters in one interview remembered the importance their mother placed on presentation. Said the elder, "At Mother's table, the plate was attractive. It had to have good color. When we got married, we couldn't select a china pattern with a plate that didn't look good with food. . . . It had to be appealing." Interestingly, their mother learned presentation skills from her mother-in-law, while her mother taught her cooking—a double legacy that has served her well.

A number of women say that the most difficult thing about learning to cook is getting everything on the table at one time. This challenge came up a number of times in the interviews. Mary G. described family dinners she cooked as a girl when her mother was serving as election judge: "I would bring the vegetable to the table, then some time later, the meat. Finally, I might bring the potato in." It took a while for her to plan so that all dishes were ready at the same time. Anne C. noted that this skill "is something you aren't taught in home economics." One young woman recounted in her interview the "trouble" she has trying to coordinate three dishes so that they are all done at the same time; she telephones her mother to get help with that. Jeanne C., who ultimately did learn as a young person the skill of coordinating food preparation, recounts her feelings: "I would have the most wonderful sense of accomplishment . . . getting things to the table on time." Part of learning to cook is learning organization and timing, and bringing them together smoothly is indeed an accomplishment.

During their time together in the kitchen, mothers pass along food-related values to their daughters, sometimes unwittingly. Even daughters who seem to their mothers not fully engaged during teaching sessions learn. Mary-Shea, interviewed with her mother Ruth, recalled, "Mom said, 'You aren't paying attention.' I *did* things, though, later, that *she* did. Her food appreciation and values influenced me as well. 'Buy organic, make it from scratch. . . . ' "

Catherine, a woman who makes excellent gravy for her friends, was greatly influenced by her mother's high standards. Gravy seems to be one food item modern women have difficulty doing well. Inexperience is part of the problem, since many cooks rarely make gravy now, except for a special holiday dinner. Some never make it. A forty-eight-year-old administrative staff person, for whom gravy is a comfort food, notes that her mother comes and cooks gravy for the daughter's family, something the daughter doesn't do herself. She laments, in fact, that "because of changing food habits, generations will grow up not knowing how to make it." Often women turn to their mothers for help when the need presents itself. Catherine offered her mother's procedure for making gravy for the benefit of readers.

## Perfect Pan Gravy
Catherine Warrick
Evelyn Jones Warrick

Catherine's note: In my family of origin, being a good cook was the most important aspect of making a good home, and my mother was a very fine cook. In her judgment, you could tell the good cooks from the poor ones by the quality of their gravy. She had especially derisive remarks to make about the sort of gravy we got when we ate out. In fact, I got to the point where I rarely ordered a meal out that included gravy in order to avoid certain disappointment.

There were several secrets to my mother's good gravy, which I dutifully observed and practiced. It isn't possible to give an actual recipe for gravy because amounts depend upon the meat drippings that result from cooking the meat of the day. Excellent gravy can be made from meat that has been either fried or roasted, if just a few points are carefully observed. As you can tell, there is as much art to this process as science, but just a little practice and patience yields the perfect gravy, whether beef, pork, chicken, or turkey.

1. It is best to make gravy in the pan in which the meat has been cooked because you lose less of the drippings. Let the drippings cool a bit, and then sprinkle about as much flour over the drippings as you have leavings

in the pan. It is better to err on the side of a little less flour in this ratio than too much. Use a wooden spoon to stir the flour and drippings together, without turning the heat on, until the mixture is smooth.

2. Next, add a cup of the liquid you are going to use to make the gravy, again stirring the mixture until very smooth. If you are going to make milk gravy, use whole milk, not reduced fat varieties. I have even used a little half-and-half in a pinch. If you want a clearer gravy, use chicken or beef broth as the liquid, depending on the type of meat you've cooked.

3. Then turn the heat to medium low under the pan, and begin adding more liquid slowly, stirring all the time as the gravy thickens. It is important to keep the mixture from getting very thick until it has heated to the bubbling point. If the mixture gets too hot when too thick, the gravy can end up with lumps in it. As the fully mixed, but still-thin gravy heats up, add salt and pepper, and/or whatever other seasonings you want to use.

4. Once the gravy has reached the boiling stage, and has started to thicken up, add more liquid until the bubbling mixture reaches the consistency that you prefer. Adding a little at a time allows you to arrive at the perfect mixture without risking a gravy that is too thin. Be certain you have the seasonings just right and adjust them if necessary. Again, it is better to add seasoning a little at a time to get it just right.

How mothers accomplish the instilling of standards varies. Suzanne Carothers writes of how African American women teach their daughters directly and indirectly, verbally and nonverbally, to give them "competency through a sense of aesthetics, an appreciation for work done beautifully: . . . Now if I go in the kitchen and say I saw these pretty biscuits, I might say [to my mother in my daughter's presence], 'Mama, how did you get these biscuits to look this pretty?' " Such indirect "instruction" is not lost on the daughter. The mothers Carothers studied have changed their culinary practices as a result of technological changes but still give their daughters chores ("real," not contrived, work) to teach them responsibility and to give them opportunities to become adept. She illustrates with the words of a thirty-two-year-old on how she mastered cooking:

Grandmama is a very good cook, and I watched her. Mama is a good cook and I watched her. I'd pick up on things. Gradually they'd let me do little things here and there. If I cooked something, I don't care what it was, they would eat it. I made some dumplings one day that were just like rubber balls! They ate them. They never complained about them. I enjoyed cooking. You know when people act like they enjoy your cooking, even when you know it's bad, you do it, and the more you do, you get better at it. I enjoyed cooking so much that I took over a lot of the cooking from Mama, especially during the week.

Carothers comments that "having chores to do was the important link bridging concrete learnings to critical understandings germane to a daughter's well-being."

Some mothers, observing their daughters' growth as they work with them in the kitchen, report a high level of engagement. In a study of psychological "flow" in motherhood, one woman is quoted as saying she achieves that optimum level of functioning and feeling "when I'm working with my daughter; when she's discovering something new [such as] a new cookie recipe that she has accomplished."

Baking seems to provide a special impetus for children to cook. Jeanne C. reports receiving miniature cooking equipment when she was a child. "The earliest Christmas present I can remember—and I don't know how old I was—five or six?—was a little girl's bake kit with little tiny boxes of cake mix and little tiny pans. . . . It was the neatest present—and it [is] the only present I remember from my childhood." Brenda Langton, long-time chef and owner of Cafe Brenda in Minneapolis, reports that every year for Christmas, she wanted a baking kit with tiny pans and mixes. Little girls' cooking equipment is as likely to be the subject of jokes as a gift nowadays. In a "Sally Forth" cartoon, Sally tells her husband about begging for a play kitchen when she was seven. "What was I thinking?"

Joke or not, some women fondly remember learning to bake, and their mother's role in that. A fifty-one-year-old writer-activist writes, "[The best thing was] the loving way she involved me in baking. I learned to love to bake." One daughter spoke to her mother during the interview: "I can remember making the Aunt Mary Christmas cookies. We saved sausage fat. . . . [I remember] your teaching us how to roll it out and chill it first." Popular food writing is full of stories of baking with Mother. Sandy Christensen, for example, tells how her mother taught her to make dilly and white batter bread when she was fourteen. Later taking a job as a chef, she now mills her own flour. Lori Beach, a woman who has been winning blue ribbons for her baked goods at the Minnesota State Fair each year for over a decade, credits her mother. "She's my inspiration. She made it fun." Carole Lalli, former editor-in-chief of *Food & Wine* magazine, began baking with her mother as a little girl and coproduced the family birthday cakes with her.

Of course, some of the worst cooking horror stories also come from baking experiences. Interestingly, these disasters often occur because respectful mothers do not hover over their daughters while they are learning to bake. In my interview with her sisters and mother, Anne C. recounted baking an angel food cake that turned out like "a high-density sponge." Anne's mother, Jean, had left her and her cooking pal, both around ten at the time, to experiment with an angel food cake mix, staying within earshot in case of emergency. The results were less than what the girls expected. Later, in high school, Anne took home economics and learned some of the basics—how to measure ingredients, for example. But, she notes, "They never taught us how to fold egg whites into a batter."

The intricacies of working with eggs figure prominently in stories of learning to bake. One woman related how her daughter failed to understand, the first time she baked meringue cookies (a family recipe), that egg whites must be beaten *before*, not *after*, combining with other ingredients. When the daughter appealed to her for help, Mother came to the rescue to make something of the "goo" that resulted.

That daughter will probably remember the support and encouragement she received, whether consciously or through increased confidence and willingness to try new things. Women do remember how their mothers responded when they tried to cook as children. Of "the best thing about my relationship with my mother," they write:

• No matter what a mess I made, she always praised my effort. She always helped me to improve. (Fifty-eight-year-old Georgian)

- She was willing to teach me and work with me as coach, cheerleader, coworker. (Thirty-eight-year-old Nebraskan)
- [The best thing was] her gentleness, willingness to do, show, help. (Massachusetts teacher's aide and homemaker)

Lillian Smith describes in a memoir her experience learning to cook with a supportive mother:

The day came when I must have my try at breaking an egg—which, somewhere in me, had become almost as taboo as setting fire to the house or flinging one of her Haviland china plates to the floor. But now I was seven and grown up enough to try and she gave her permission. I stood trembling for five minutes on the edge of that precipice before I could take the fatal step. But I took it. I cracked the egg. Then hesitating again, I brought on disaster by spilling the egg on the floor. But Mother did not scold: she said, "It happens; let's clean it up." We cleaned it up. Then she said, "Try again." And I tried again and did it. And I am not sure any triumph in my life ever pleased me more than that successful act.

Children's experience learning to cook appears to affect their experience with food as adults. Two-thirds of the women surveyed like to cook. Enjoying cooking as an adult correlates with having learned about cooking by being in the kitchen, by watching Mother cook, and by being taught to cook. Women who enjoy cooking, in turn, are more likely to believe their current diet is healthy.

In her study of women, eating, and identity, Kim Chernin recounts the story of how, as a child, the great food writer M.F.K. Fisher made a pudding that turned out to be poisonous to her allergic mother. Fisher's mother subsequently comforted her daughter from her own sickbed, saying, "Don't worry, sweet . . . it was the loveliest pudding I have ever seen." Chernin attributes Fisher's "lifelong fascination with cooking" in part to her mother's sensitive response on this occasion.

Knowing how to provide meals for oneself and others is fundamental to life. It confers a certain independence, grounded in self-reliance. A thirty-nine-year-old educator learned this by observing her spouse's struggles with cooking: "My husband knows nothing about cooking, and although he tries, he has trouble with very basic recipes. I see that I learned a basic life skill from my mother that he lacks. . . ." As women like this one realize the value of whatever they learned from Mother about food, they reflect appreciatively. A twenty-nine-year-old Michigan woman offers simply this: "She tried to make sure I could take care of myself."

## BARRIERS TO LEARNING FROM MOTHER

Some women do not learn practical cooking skills from their mothers. Eleven percent of women surveyed report that their mothers cooked, but did not teach them anything. One woman in her eighties, a marvelous cook with fond memories of her mother as a "wonderful cook," says, "I can't remember a thing I learned about cooking from my mother except that good, substantial, simple food was . . . basic, . . . the most important thing that you can do for your family." Of course, this is no trivial piece of learning—just not practical!

Even within the same family, mother-to-daughter teaching about food may be vastly different. Beverly, in her sixties, comments, "My mother wouldn't let us near a stove." Her daughter Kevlyn, on the other hand, learned a great deal in her mother's kitchen. When Kevlyn left the family home, in fact, Beverly could no longer give a party without hiring help, since she had depended on Kevlyn's help. Now Kevlyn contrasts what she learned from her mother with what her own children are learning from her: "As an only child, I helped. I haven't been as good with my children. I find it easier to get the dinner alone."

Why is it that some daughters learn from their mothers, while others don't? First, and most obviously, some mothers do not cook. Four percent of women in the survey sample had mothers in this category. Perhaps these mothers are like Norma Jean and Carole Darden's Aunt Lil, who "loathes cooking and admits it!" "Sorry, Dearie, I can't even remember how to cook," she said, when they asked her for contributions to their family cookbook and memoir. A forty-four-year-old Californian regrets that her mother did not cook, because of the "lack of opportunity for the two of us to bond as mothers and homemakers." As the oldest of five children, this woman began to cook for her siblings when she was about eleven years old, teaching herself as she went along.

Otherwise, her mother kept only "sandwich fixings" in the house for family meals.

Other reasons than the mother's lack of cooking may apply, however. Some families have a paid cook. Such was the case in the childhood home of a retired Louisiana newspaperwoman: "Food just wasn't that big a deal. Mama did the shopping, bought the best, and Birdie cooked it superbly. That was the way life was." Ruth Reichl, editor of *Gourmet* and former chef, apparently discovered fine food from both live-in cooks and travel abroad; she memorialized her own mother's poor cooking in "The Queen of Mold," a chapter of her memoir *Tender at the Bone* ("My mission was to keep Mom from killing anybody who came to dinner"). In other families, the father did the cooking. A sixty-seven-year-old retired nurse practitioner writes, "Mother had the education, and, during the Depression, she was the bread winner. She worked, and my father did most of the cooking."

In most households, however, mothers do the cooking. Why some mothers do not invite children into the kitchen, or encourage them when they are there, bears comment. It illuminates, for one thing, what the experience of cooking is like for some women. A few survey respondents write that their mothers found meal preparation extremely stressful, as noted in Chapter 3. Harried as they were, such women, many just finishing a workday and now facing meal preparation for the family, might be loath to have children in the kitchen. Some of the learning that daughters get in such circumstances, then, turns out to be about how stressful cooking can be.

Lack of patience on the mother's part, no doubt related in many instances to stress, is cited as another reason daughters do not learn to cook. One woman comments, "I think my mother was just impatient." Other women in their fifties perceived this as well. A Georgia administrative assistant comments, "She was not patient enough to teach me to cook. She gave me more of the clean-up chores, so I had to learn on my own once I got married." A homemaker-teacher from New Mexico notes that her mother "has always prided herself on her cooking skills. It has meant a great deal to her. But she did not have the patience to teach me." Lack of patience may be behind the anger one mother reportedly showed when she tried to teach her daughter how to cook. The child "quickly lost interest."

Sometimes mothers' perfectionism, need to control the outcome, or desire to avoid a mess, prevents them from allowing children to participate. Indeed, some mothers do not want (or even allow) children in the kitchen. A twenty-five-year-old college senior writes that her grandmother never allowed her mother or the other children in the kitchen because "she feared they would hurt themselves." A forty-five-year-old project manager recalls of her mother, "She wouldn't let me cook with her." Her mother would say, "I don't like anybody in the kitchen when I'm cooking. I don't like people helping me." Similarly, a fifty-five-year-old nonprofit administrator remembers that her mother rarely let her cook. "She didn't like messes. She was very uptight about entertaining—wanting everything to be perfect." Some daughters believe that their mothers compete with them in cooking. In Judith Arcana's study of mothers and daughters, food comes up as an arena where competition rears its head. "My mother always had to feel that she did things better than I did" is one woman's way of expressing this.

These barriers to a favorable environment for learning to cook may be covered or hidden sometimes by comments such as "The kitchen was Mother's domain," or "That's her bailiwick." The element of control may indeed be a factor, for, as anthropologists of food have observed, "control of food across history and cultures has often been a key source of power for women." But more positive factors may be at work as well. Cooking is one of the more enjoyable responsibilities women have at home. Psychologist Mihaly Csikszentmihalyi found in his study of people's feelings during daily activities that "cooking is often a positive experience" for women. Since it constitutes a source of pleasure for many women, they may want to enjoy that pleasure free of other responsibilities, such as teaching, guiding, and monitoring helpers.

Preparing meals may also fill a need for solitude and serve as a way to exercise creativity. The kitchen has often been the only room women could claim as their own. Women have some of their best moods in the kitchen, "where they are in control and involved in cooking." This is especially important since women have traditionally been "expected" to cook. Cleaning the kitchen, on the other hand, is "generally among the most negative experiences" for women, according to Csikszentmihalyi. This may be one reason they are more willing or eager for children to be involved in noncooking aspects of providing meals, such as setting the table or washing the dishes. One daughter of three interviewed with their mother referred to a "detailed schedule of chores" such as these in her family.

Looking back on what their mothers offered—and could have offered—fills some women with regret that they couldn't, or didn't, learn more. Four percent report that not learning from their mothers—or not learning anything *useful*—was the worst thing in their food connection with their mothers (the same proportion whose mothers did not cook). But these mothers were not always completely responsible for a lack of learning. Some tried to teach their daughters but saw their efforts thwarted. Bobbie Ann Mason writes in her memoir *Clear Springs* that her mother tells her now, "You didn't want to learn. . . . You had your nose in a book." A twenty-two-year-old Michigan college student, on the other hand, writes that she resisted her mother's efforts to teach her to cook because she felt she was sometimes pushed too hard to learn.

Whatever the reason, some daughters wish they had taken advantage of their mothers' cooking knowledge when they had the opportunity. A woman in her forties expresses this sentiment: "I wish I had spent more time baking and cooking with her, and I wish I had paid closer attention to her skills and talents. I took for granted that she would always be there to call for a recipe or advice. Mothers are very special!" Having let the opportunity pass to get instruction from my mother on certain specialties of hers, I have the same feeling. While they are still able to help, I have been asking other female elders in my family to tell me how to cook Mama's creamed white corn and fried chicken, dishes I've never made but now want to.

## LEARNING WHEN MOTHER IS NOT CLOSE AT HAND

Many women, like Carol, quoted above, had mothers who were in the kitchen a great deal. And my best times, often my only concentrated times, with my mother were in the kitchen. But such time was limited, since she worked a long day. Like Mama, many mothers work outside the home now. Though they may not have as much time in the kitchen as do those who work at home, they nevertheless teach their daughters some things about cooking. It was my job from time to time, for example, to drain the soaking dried navy beans when I got home from school, add water and a piece of ham or salt pork (we called it *streak o' lean*) and put the pot on the stove to simmer. My mother then used the beans as the basis for a meal when she got home some three hours later. I needed to watch the beans, making sure the water did not evaporate completely, thereby causing the beans to stick to the bottom of the pot. Mama told me just how much water to add when the beans began to get too dry. She taught me to recognize when they had cooked to our standard of doneness and to turn the heat off when that time came. It was in this way that I learned how to cook dried beans, while advancing our family dinner preparation.

Jeanne C. took more responsibility than I, though not alone. She and her grandmother kept the house running while her mother worked. She remembers: "When I was ten, I started doing the cooking during the week. Mom would do a lot of stuff on the weekend so there would be things pre-fixed, but then I'd have to set the table and start things so that when she got home . . . we could have dinner."

The working mother phenomenon goes back further than the forties and fifties of Jeanne's childhood, and mine. Women my mother's age had working mothers as well. Kathleen, a seventy-eight-year-old who grew up in rural Wisconsin, spoke of her experience in our interview: "My mother worked. My dad died when I was young. . . . She'd set stuff out, then I'd come home from school and do that cooking. My brother learned, too, from that. Mom didn't come home until after six o'clock. So we learned that way. We took turns. We cooked what Mom said to cook. Then she would correct us and say, 'You should've done thus and so.' So it was hands-on, but still finding out from Mom what we did wrong. Then we corrected that."

Their inability to teach their daughters directly pains some modern American working mothers. Beatrice Pesquera shows, in her work on Chicana women, how many of them are torn between their desire to teach their daughters and the realities of their lives. Even though these women believe it is their job to teach their daughters how to make tortillas and *chili verde*, their work outside the home makes that very difficult. Some of these mothers, then, try to find "tortilla grandmas" to provide *la cultura*, including culinary skills, for their children.

These examples suggest how working mothers can provide teaching for their daughters *in absentia* or by proxy. The daughters' efforts can then contribute to family meals or, in such cases as Kathleen's, provide the basis for an entire meal.

As suggested earlier, grandmothers figure as cooking teachers, too. One group of sisters recalled their grandmother "Cracker's" fudge: "Her fudge was truly one of the greatest things. Mine never tasted right. I got her to stand with me and make it. I apprenticed. Now I can make it." A woman who grew up in a large family recalled in her interview how her grandmother, crippled with arthritis, taught her and other grandchildren to make traditional strudel:

I learned to make what [my mother] didn't teach, which was strudel and kolaches, from my grandmother. She had a little high-rise apartment downtown. . . . Those little apartments, honestly, the stove was this big [gesture to show a narrow width], and I remember we went down there. She was going to teach us to make strudel. She took the German strudel recipe from [my mother's dad's family]. There were fifteen or sixteen people in this tiny place, so she didn't cut the recipe in half. Here we were in this little high-rise apartment, and we opened and draped her dining room table. As she worked, her hands were like large knobs. She had arthritis, and she could hardly stand at the time, she was so crippled with arthritis, but she still baked. I'm sure at the time she hadn't made a strudel for years. But on this table laid out with a cloth, she started with this blob of dough, and then she worked. It was a little miracle the way she made the dough thinner and thinner and thinner, all along telling us, "You tear it, you start over. It's no good." [You work] until it's just as thin as can be, but it's also the size of the table! And then you add the fillings and do the roll-up. This thing was so huge we couldn't get it on to a cookie sheet. But she wanted it *whole*. She didn't want us to cut it in half. The way it's made is *whole*. Well, we couldn't get it in the oven because the apartment ovens were these little teeny things. It slopped over the sides, but we finally got it in. I'm sure it was ten pounds of strudel.

As she told this story, this granddaughter's delight shone. Clearly, she admired her grandmother's skill and high standards of performance, and she values knowing how to do things her grandmother did. It is important to some young women to learn the way grandmother does things with food. Lillian Smith writes in *The Journey* that, as "Little Grandma" told stories, "we would be roasting pecans in the ashes, or sweet potatoes—because we knew that potatoes had been cooked that way, when she was young, and we wanted to try things the way she had done them."

Though grandmothers who live long lives may continue to help their adult granddaughters develop their cooking skills, for many married women, mothers-in-law play that role. The timing is right, for one thing. Women often begin cooking when they marry, and the mother-in-law may be more accessible than the mother, grandmother, or other women of their birth family. A forty-seven-year-old Michigan woman illustrates:

I married at age twenty-four and feel that my husband and I grew up together. . . . He and his family taught me most of the positive "kitchen" wisdom I have. I met his Italian grandmother several years before she died (when she still was accustomed to making her own pastas, sauces, pizzas). His mother is still living and in good health, [while] my mother died when I was thirty-nine [after over a decade of illness]. I never got to know my parents as an adult.

Women whose birth mothers *are* available nevertheless pick up good tips from their mothers-in-law, such as these Martha got about making gravy: "If you add any water, make it potato water. When you cook the meat, put a few dried mushrooms in it."

Some women learn from women completely outside the family. Young people's organizations provide one type of opportunity. A thirty-nine-year-old Texan, whose mother cooked little, writes of starting to cook first as a Brownie, then as a Girl Scout—for a badge. Her mother supported these efforts, as did the mother of a Nebraska human service professional, who went with her daughter to 4H, where the daughter "took many cooking classes."

The formal cooking classes I took as a youngster were in school. Due to a move between eighth and ninth grades, and cross-district curriculum differences, I was required to take home economics twice. These classes gave me a chance to learn and practice, in a structured way, the fundamentals of cooking and sewing, both of which I have used throughout my life. Home economics teachers provide many youngsters a foundation in preparing food, and sometimes even a specialty. Kevlyn recalled having such a teacher in junior high. The teacher liked to make pies. "I was her aide for a couple of years, and I really got a love for making pies." Kevlyn subsequently developed into a baker and recalls "making tiered cakes for people before I was thirteen."

But it is possible to learn to cook without mentoring and teaching by other people. I maintain that anyone can cook who can read and follow directions, based on my own experience cooking from cookbooks and recipes. And that is what inexperienced women in my study did when circumstances or desire compelled them to cook on their own. They worked from recipes and cookbooks, supplemented sometimes by advice or clarifications from their mothers and others.

In addition to teaching her how to do some cooking, such as making gravy (see recipe earlier in this chapter), Catherine's mother gave her the *American Home All-Purpose Cookbook* as a Christmas gift when she was in her mid-thirties. The gentle inscription reads, "To my daughter Cathy . . . not because she isn't a good cook but because she may wish to improve her already excellent ability. With love, Mom." That cookbook was her mother's favorite, and she wanted Catherine to have one. Natalie, a daughter whose mother wrote a cookbook, partly for her three daughters' benefit, testified to the importance of that cookbook in both inspiring her and helping her learn to cook: "Because the food was really wonderful here growing up, having the recipes in this book made it easier."

Learners strive to make recipes turn out, and experiment as well, appealing to Mother or other elders for help when they get in a spot. Jean said, in an interview with her three daughters, "When I got married, I knew little. . . . I would try something. If I had trouble, I would call either my mother or my mother-in-law and ask them. I liked to struggle on. I scanned recipe books." A forty-two-year-old liturgist used her mother's expertise in a more formal way as she learned. She made her mother's recipes "with Mom around for mastering the tricks and shortcuts not always written down, and/or [I made a recipe] and took it home for her to evaluate for my improvement."

Judy told of her transition to becoming a cook. She lived at home with her parents until she graduated from college, then established a home with her husband and began to cook. "I can tell you the first thing I made—beef Stroganoff. . . . I had no idea what it was! We were having three bachelors to dinner. I figured out if I could read a recipe I could do it. I made it, and they loved it. I can still read a recipe and figure out if it's going to be worthwhile, for the most part."

Anecdotal evidence suggests that some cooks today are so in-experienced that cookbook writers must include many more de-tails in recipes than were required in the past. Marje Jaasma, a California college communication teacher, told me that her stu-dents notice this in perusing cookbooks. She uses the term *low context communication* to describe the phenomenon "because the whole message needs to be spelled out." Cookbook writers are unable to assume the reader/user of the cookbook has basic cook-ing knowledge, so they write instructions for procedures that were common knowledge in earlier years. One food industry expert confirms this trend, reporting "a growing . . . cooking illiteracy. . . . People are calling us for basic information on how to cook; they don't have the cooking skills they need to have." She reports this phenomenon becomes especially apparent at holiday times. How widespread is the problem of cooking illiteracy is difficult to say. As noted earlier, most women say they prepare meals regularly; sixty-three percent judge themselves to be competent cooks.

A cookbook that has helped many women learn to cook is Irma S. Rombauer's *The Joy of Cooking*, first published in 1931. It is the third best-selling cookbook of all time and was reissued in its original form in 1998, the "All New All Purpose" version having been introduced in 1997. The late food writer and novelist Laurie Colwin said, "Mrs. Rombauer is to food what Dr. Spock is to ba-bies." One woman, Elizabeth P. Foster, told a food writer that, when she married at twenty-five, she "couldn't cook an entire meal." Her husband asked his sister, a home economics teacher, to buy a cookbook for his new wife. The sister chose *The Joy of Cooking*. Foster reported that she quoted "my friend, Irma," when she talked about cooking. Jenny, who spent three years in England during college, remarked in our interview that, besides calling her mother for help with cooking, she "got the *Joy of Cooking*."

I consider Irma Rombauer my own friend as well, along with her daughter, Marion Rombauer Becker, who, as an adult, worked with her mother on the book. When I graduated from college, a friend of my mother's I call "my fairy godmother" sent me *The Joy of Cooking*. Virginia Black was a career home economist, and she knew food. When I began to cook in more than a casual way, I realized what a gold mine *Joy* is. Were I reduced to only one cookbook (and I have and use many cookbooks), this would be the one. I could live four lives and never try all the recipes in it. (Like Laurie Colwin's, mine is held together with duct tape, having been so heavily used.) I learn from it every time I use it and give the book as both a wedding and a graduation gift. It's an invaluable resource.

## DAUGHTER-TO-MOTHER LEARNING

Conventionally, our conception of the direction of learning is that of mother to daughter, but learning goes both ways between the two. Research suggests that, just as mothers influence daughters, so daughters influence mothers. This is as true in food-related matters as in others. Many mothers are well aware of how their daughters have influenced them. One woman told a food writer, "I really think my girls have taught me to be creative and to change." My own mother learned a few things from me, such as adding garbanzo beans to her repertoire of dried beans to use in salads, soups, and casseroles. She loved to eat at my table and marveled that I could cook, since much of my learning happened out of her purview.

Some women with adult daughters tell of learning from them tips on shopping and cooking for the conditions of modern life. When my sister-in-law Barbara took a job outside the home, for example, her daughter Bonnie encouraged her to save dinner preparation time by buying peeled and cut carrots, rather than processing them herself. All mothers interviewed report learning something from their daughters—what the current crop of young children likes to eat; how to bake yeast bread (especially from daughters who came of age in the sixties and seventies); how to feed a vegetarian; how to prepare food in healthier ways; and how to buy and use new foods or cuisines (from moves to different parts of the country or world). Beverly recounted how her daughter's move to California introduced her to Asian foods and new lettuces. Judy told about Heidi's teaching her to make quesadillas.

Kathleen E. was especially vocal about the things she's learned from her daughter, Jeanne E. "She has taught me times have changed. We don't have to do the traditional thing." She related then the story of a family event for which she thought roasting a turkey was most appropriate. Jeanne persuaded her to get honey-baked ham instead. "It was delicious," declared the mother. She admitted that she "wouldn't have thought of that." When Jeanne says, on more ordinary occasions, "I'll pick up a pizza," Kathleen says normally she's "not thinking that way." But she has learned to appreciate the options. And she admires Jeanne's artful ways with food: "When the family comes to her house for Christmas, . . . we know it's going to be gourmet."

One generational change is the rise of vegetarianism. Vegetarian daughters have an almost unavoidable impact on their mothers. Although a few such daughters I surveyed write of how their mothers tried to sabotage their choice by sneaking meat into their food or "forgetting" their daughters' commitment to a vegetarian diet, mothers tend to work to accommodate their daughters' vegetarianism. Still, it involves some adjusting and learning for all concerned. Kate L. spoke of how becoming a vegetarian was "a deviation from the norm." Her family has always placed a high value on food and coming together around it. In the past, family meals included meat. Now, when invited to dinner at either parent's home (her parents are now divorced and remarried), Kate feels pressure to announce early whether she's coming because a menu has to be planned to accommodate her. "I'm the exception. They could have a pork chop, but because I'm coming, it's stifling the natural flow of the meal. . . . There's an unspoken 'problem.' " But Mary M., Kate's mother, says she has learned a great deal from Kate's vegetarianism. One of the things she's attended to is how Kate has chosen to take care of herself. Another is the "absolutely wonderful food" Kate cooks. Kate's vegetarianism has influenced the nature of the meals in her mother's home as well as in her own. Mary noted, "We have a whole repertoire of vegetarian foods that we prepare now. [My stepdaughter] just brought home a vegetarian boyfriend, and it was just totally comfortable."

Other mothers, in reflecting what they have learned, tell how their daughters bring new dishes to the family cooking repertoire. When I asked Jean for a family recipe for this book after an interview with her three daughters, she gave me this one for red-hot macaroni and cheese. Her oldest daughter, Anne C., adapted a recipe she found in a cookbook for macaroni and cheese in a way that has made it a family favorite. Anne's final sentence in the instructions reflects something she said in the interview: "I never *cook* my dinner; I *heat* it." A single woman, Anne cooks "for friends and the freezer."

## Red-hot Macaroni and Cheese
Anne Clark

Anne's note: You can double, but not triple, this recipe. Three times this amount is too much to handle.

Boil 8 minutes in salted water, then drain:

1 pound medium elbow macaroni

In a Dutch oven, melt:

⅓ cup margarine or butter

Add:

1 medium finely chopped onion (about ⅔ cup), stirring until soft.

Blend in ⅓ cup flour and cook until bubbly.

Gradually pour in:

2¼ cups milk
1 cup half-and-half, slowly stirring.

Continue to cook and stir until sauce thickens. (Use whisk.)

Reduce heat and add:

1 teaspoon crushed dried red chili peppers
1 teaspoon Worcestershire sauce

Stir in:

1 pound sharp cheddar cheese, cubed
½ cup dry white wine
salt and pepper to taste

Add:

1 red bell pepper, diced

1 green bell pepper, diced

1 (or 1½) cans diced green chili peppers

Add:

cubed ham or Canadian bacon (to taste)

cooked macaroni

Check seasoning. Serve, or package for the freezer and reheat for subsequent meals.

Daughters who follow their mothers in choosing professions that center on food offer a special resource to their mothers. Ann Caron quotes a mother whose daughter is a chef. "Even though I've been in the food business for years, I now defer to her in the kitchen. It's wonderful—we call and exchange recipes." But many mothers defer to adult daughters in the kitchen even when the daughter is not a food professional. Roles in the kitchen may switch. *Mothers* may help or clean up. One twenty-four-year-old Virginian describes an evolving role for her mother as she gained competence and confidence as a cook: "As I grew older, I would hate to have her help me cook in the kitchen. Now she is just my apprentice—to peel, chop, shred, and wash the dishes in the end!" Other mothers, unable, or unwilling, to adopt the apprentice or helper role when the daughter is in charge, may become so annoying in their behavior that they are banished from the kitchen. One woman in her seventies told how she came to kick her mother out of the kitchen: "Mom lived with us after I married and had children. We'd be in the kitchen together and she'd say, 'Oh, you don't want *that*,' or 'Let's put caraway in this.' Finally, when I got to be forty, and we were having Thanksgiving dinner, I said, 'Mom, *out*!' and I cooked my own dinner. She was hurt. She cried, and I felt bad. . . . She thought she was helping. I had five children, and she was helping."

But mothers who are open to change can learn from daughters.

That they do is not surprising. For one thing, times change. A majority of women report eating a wider range of foods now than they did in their childhood home (70 percent strongly agree or agree on the survey) and cooking differently than did their mothers (63 percent strongly agree or agree). A series of "Stone Soup" cartoons deals with cooking differences in the generations. The mother of young daughters insists *her* live-in mother not use fish sticks, marshmallows, or Jell-O when she cooks for them. Mother replies "But I don't *do* tofu." The girls *like* marshmallows, so they're very positive about Grandma's way of cooking, especially when she compromises by topping vegetable dishes with a marshmallow sauce!

Some mothers interviewed spoke of learning from young daughters. One related how she's learned to let her small daughter, Kate E., regulate her own eating: "Kate's not overtly lactose intolerant . . . but she's never liked milk and cheese. They give her a sour stomach. There's a reason for the way she eats. Our pediatrician friend says, 'Leave her alone.' She eats . . . other things that do agree with her. So there's . . . self-selecting. Leaving her alone is the best thing." Nutritionist Eleanor Eckstein's review of research lends support for this pediatrician's approach. She concludes that a laissez-faire approach that avoids control but encourages trying new foods "is likely to lead to an open-minded, flexible approach to food." Jacqueline related how, the very day of our interview, she and her daughter Jolawn, a sixteen-year-old athlete concerned with her performance, visited a nutritionist to analyze Jolawn's food intake. Jacqueline remarked, "[The nutritionist] said, out of all the persons who had done the nutritional analysis, Jolawn's essentially turned out the healthiest, the best. I was surprised, because as a mother I'm constantly saying, 'Eat your veggies,' and 'Make sure that you have enough protein.' But Jolawn was right on target when it came to protein and just a little under when it came to carbohydrates and vegetables.' "

Jolawn and Jacqueline's experience also demonstrates how young daughters can bring new dishes to the family repertoire. Jolawn taught her mother the enjoyment of pasta other than spaghetti. "She'll come in after a game and simply do pasta sprinkled with cheese." Jolawn spent six weeks in France the year before our interview and learned to make crêpes while there. When she came home, she introduced them to her family. Now, according to Jacqueline, "For special occasions, we do a dessert with crêpes as a base, and strawberries. It is just delightful."

Forty-five percent of women responding to the survey believe they've influenced their mothers in some way about food. Healthier, lighter foods are most often mentioned as an influence, at 23 percent of total responses ("more veggie items"; "tofu and tempeh"; "organic stuff"), followed by wider variety of foods ("different herbs and spices") at 22.4 percent. Next come special recipes at 22.1 percent and cooking techniques ("less fat"; "bake or broil more foods"; "steam veggies") at 17 percent. The blessings of take-out and more easily prepared foods are next, at 4 percent ("It's okay to eat fast food or use prepared foods occasionally"; "Take out isn't all bad"). Perhaps the most delightful response, though, was "How to make crème brulée at home with a butane torch."

Learning about food is a two-way street between mothers and daughters. Daughters learn from mothers, if the opportunity and openness are there, and mothers learn from daughters, under the same conditions. What may be learned ranges from values to specific cooking techniques. How learning takes place varies as well, from direct training to simply being in the presence of cooking. The strength of women's memories of their learning testifies to its importance. Food is fundamental to life. There is always something to learn, and the mother-daughter bond offers a lifelong opportunity to do so. For many mothers and daughters, that opportunity is an ongoing gift.

# 5

# "As If Nutrition Were Enough": Food for the Circumstances of Life

About the time I started working on this book, my husband took to his bed feeling sick. I gave him the food and drink my mother would have offered for his condition—ginger ale, soda crackers, and clear broth. Later, when I telephoned the nurse on duty at our health clinic to talk over his illness and ask what to do for him, she suggested what I had already done—virtually the same practices as my own mother's of half a century ago.

This reminded me that, besides the everyday uses of food, mothers come forward with food in special circumstances. They offer us food not only for nourishment, but for healing, comfort, welcome, and celebration. In all these circumstances, food stands as a symbol of nurture. This chapter explores some of the ways mothers accomplish this and what it means to their daughters.

## FOOD FOR ILLNESS

In his book *Domesticity*, food writer Bob Shacochis writes of how his partner learned from her mother how to treat herself when she was sick, including what to feed herself. He describes how this mother cared for her daughter when she was ailing as a child—spreading a terrycloth towel out on her pillow, "irrigating" her with unlimited ginger ale and, later, when she was better, feeding her milk toast. Mothers know a lot about how to care for sick people. Cokie Roberts recounts how she and her peers at work function for young coworker mothers much as older family women did in earlier times. They provide advice that is essentially the same as that of health professionals. "After a few times of hearing both me and the doctor say things like 'Cheese, bananas, and rice,' the young women [whose children have stomachaches] stop bothering the doctor and just check in with the experienced mothers." A twenty-year-old New Jersey woman confirms this capacity of mothers to know what to do for a sick child, writing, "Whenever I was down or sick, my mother always knew the right foods to make me better." Historian Julia Cherry Spruill's work documents European American women's practice of searching out and preparing food and drink for the ill of the household from the earliest colonial period.

Eighty-two percent of survey respondents remember their mothers usually giving them special food and drink when they were sick, with 80 still taking that food and drink at least some of the time when they are sick and giving it to their own children or other sick people in their care. Asked to name the particular food and drink their mothers gave them, cross-generational women respond in surprisingly uniform ways. Of the items named by these women, a total of over 1100, the most common are soups (usually chicken soup), at 25 percent. (Chicken soup has been on the menu for the sick for so long that it has prompted a few scientific studies, which support its use for flu and colds.) After soup comes carbonated beverages (usually ginger ale or Coke) at 17 percent; toast at 10 percent; and crackers (usually saltines) and tea, each at 9 percent. Eighty-nine percent of respondents named at least one food or drink item their mother gave them during illness. Rounding out the top ten food and drink items offered in sickness are various fruit juices, Jell-O, frozen treats such as Popsicles and ice cream, eggs and egg dishes, and cocoa. Some survey and interview participants mentioned the BRAT diet (bananas, rice, applesauce, toast) for diarrhea. Apparently no longer common, and infrequently mentioned, remedies from earlier in the century include various concoctions of spirits— hot toddies, blackberry brandy, hot beer with milk and sugar, and bourbon with sugar.

Within the usual categories of sick food, children have their own preferences, and mothers go to some length to accommodate those preferences when they are not readily available. Anne C., who grew up in Minnesota, recalled how, when she had mononucleosis in February one year, her mother Jean searched Minneapolis grocery stores to find grape Popsicles. Sometimes mothers prepare special treats in the kitchen for sick children. Cokie Roberts reports how, when she was sick as a child, her mother whipped up floating island, "a custard with islands of meringue floating on top," her favorite dessert. A 40-year-old says she still fixes herself a big custard when she is recovering from illness. Her mother gave custard to her youngsters during recuperation, believing the nutrition in it was restorative. Similar beliefs hold for bread pudding and rice pudding.

Not only the food itself, but special presentation of it, makes an impression on daughters during illness. One of the sweetest stories told in interviews was that of a pair of daughters recalling their mother's care during times of illness. "We had a little bell," remembered one, indicating how the sick children could signal their mother from the sickbed when they needed her. Looking at their mother, the other daughter said, "I stayed in bed. You'd bring my lunch and breakfast up and put it on a bed table." Mary M. remembers her mother bringing her "treats on a tray, including a flower," when she was sick as a child. A 61-year-old Pennsylvania writer notes that the food wasn't necessarily special. "What mattered was that she used her best dishes and made sickroom trays an aesthetic experience."

## COMFORT FOOD

Related to food given in illness is food given to comfort. The concept of comfort food, though commonplace (three-fourths of women surveyed report the term evokes thoughts for them), is a bit elusive, since it means different things to different people. I tried to get at the nature of comfort food by asking survey participants if their mothers gave them particular food after a hard day or a disappointment, and if so, what. Then I asked if the term *comfort food* had any meaning for them, and if so, to list such food. An Illinois college student thinks of comfort food as "food that has special meaning, not necessarily used to make me feel better." Another, writing of tomato soup and chicken noodle soup ("We ate that a lot"), remembers such food as exemplifying "pleasure and safety."

In one interview, sisters Lisa and Lynn talked about food their mother Marlyn provided for them during periods of "finicky eating," or when she and her spouse were to be out for dinner. Creamed tuna on soda crackers and macaroni and cheese were two dishes they named, both dubbed "bunny food" by their paternal grandmother, a name subsequently adopted by the entire family. Their story reminds me that food writer Laurie Colwin writes of "nursery food," rather than of comfort food; her examples overlap considerably with the comfort foods adult women name.

One woman, interviewed with her daughter, both of whom love eating, said, "Any food is comfort food!" But comfort food clearly connects to Mother for some women. A 44-year-old commented in her interview, "To me it's direct connection with mother and home. It's home cooking. It's a direct line that provides comfort like mother." What is true for her is apparently true for other women as well. Of the comfort foods named by survey respondents, 73 percent are (or were) cooked by their mothers.

For me, such dishes as macaroni and cheese, Crowder peas and cornbread, and grilled cheese sandwiches with tomato soup constitute comfort food. It's significant that I do not often cook these foods or order them in restaurants, and, in that, I am like other women whose comfort foods are more about memory than about current diet. Since I no longer live in the South, some of my comfort foods are harder to come by. They are comfort food for me *as my mother cooked them*, "transformed by love and memory," in the words of Sarah Breathnach. Some survey respondents, likewise, write that they do not eat the foods now that they regard as comfort foods. *Someone* is eating comfort food, though, as evidenced by the increase in restaurant menus featuring "home cooking" and cookbooks dedicated to comfort food, such as *The Homespun Cookbook: Comfort Food Favorites from the Heart of America* and *The Comfort Food Cookbook*. And I admit that, since writing this chapter, having been reminded of my own comfort foods, I've been buying and making tomato soup more than usual!

Survey results present a snapshot of women's comfort food favorites. Baked sweets of various sorts made the best showing on the list, at 15 percent of all comfort foods named. Included in this category are cookies, brownies, pie, pastries, and cake. This finding surprised me a bit, perhaps because I do not view baked sweets as comfort food. But its association with another finding—that women's memories baking with their mothers appear to top all other memories of cooking together—makes it more understandable.

The next most frequently named comfort foods in the survey are meat dishes, such as meatloaf, pot roast, beef stew, and corned beef with cabbage (14 percent). Soup, especially chicken soup, came in third at 11 percent. "Homemade vegetable" and tomato soup are specified as well. Dian Eversole is a woman who has for several years given dinners for fifteen to sixty people every second Sunday of the month, to build community and stay in touch with her friends. She reports that the only meal she's ever served more than once is cream of tomato soup and grilled cheese sandwiches. She prepares this meal, the group's "very favorite," every winter.

Potatoes, especially mashed potatoes and gravy, and pasta/noodle dishes each account for 8 percent of survey responses. One woman names three potato dishes as her comfort foods and writes in the survey margin, "Hey, we're Irish!" Some women think of potato salad as a comfort food. When asked to contribute a recipe to this book, Carol offered this one.

## Carol's Potato Salad

Carol Earnshaw Holmberg
Beverly Pike Earnshaw
Paula Heinrich Pike

Carol's note: I remember my mother making this dish for all family picnics and special occasions, especially those which required "comfort food" to ease the soul. Mother told me that her German mother, Paula Heinrich, taught her to make this dish the "German way" by mixing the potatoes and eggs with all other ingredients while the eggs and potatoes are very warm. One has to work very rapidly, but it's worth it! I always chill the salad before serving, but it can certainly be served warm, also.

For 12 servings:

## Main ingredients

6 to 8 medium red or white potatoes

1 dozen eggs

1 cup diced sweet onion

1 cup diced celery

fresh herbs of your choice (chives are especially good)

2 cups salad dressing (recipe below)

To begin main ingredients: Place potatoes (peeled or unpeeled) in cold water to cover on stove, bring to a boil, and boil on medium heat until done, about 30 minutes. Place eggs in cold water, bring to boil, and boil on medium heat 15 minutes. While eggs and potatoes are cooking, make salad dressing in mixer.

## Salad dressing ingredients

2 egg yolks

2 tablespoons sugar

1 teaspoon dry mustard

¼ teaspoon paprika

1 teaspoon kosher salt

2 tablespoons vinegar

2 cups peanut oil

2 tablespoons lemon juice

Place the 2 raw egg yolks in mixer bowl, and beat until thick at medium speed for 1 minute. Add sugar, dry mustard, paprika, and kosher salt to egg yolks and beat at medium speed 30 seconds. Scrape bowl, if needed. Add vinegar slowly to egg mixture, continuing at medium speed, and stop when mixed.

Pour two cups of peanut oil into measuring cup with a spout, and turn mixer speed to medium. Pour oil in thin stream into egg mixture until dressing is thick and creamy, 2 minutes or more. Continue beating, adding lemon juice gradually to the mixture. Beat 1 minute longer. Put aside. (Author's note: Some of the dressing can be kept for future use.)

Putting it all together: When potatoes are cooked sufficiently so that a fork slides through them easily, remove from heat. Peel, if needed. Remove eggs from heat after 15 minutes' boiling time. Cube potatoes and chop eggs into very large mixing bowl, working quickly, so that potatoes and eggs stay very warm as you add onion, celery, herbs, and salad dressing. Test the flavor, adding salt, pepper, etc., to taste. Place in serving bowl and sprinkle with paprika. Cover and place in refrigerator.

Not all comfort foods are carbohydrates and meats. One interviewed woman remarked, "My association with the largesse of the family is more garden produce, strawberries, asparagus—food to be anticipated with a lot of relish." Another named both fresh vegetables from the garden and corncakes. Like other women who grew up in the South, or with Southern family background, this woman's comfort food has a decidedly Southern flavor. Some comfort food does have a regional or ethnic flavor. Accordingly, many African American and Southern white women name such dishes as fried chicken, turnip greens, yams, cornbread, and catfish; Hispanic women name *carnitas, menudo, posole, mole*, mashed tara root, *natillas*, tamales, and green *chile* and beans; Norwegian women name potato cakes; and other foods associated with family heritage, such as Dutch vegetable soup, kugel, and manicotti, make their appearance.

Tea is by far the most-named "liquid" response to the invitation to list comfort foods, drawing nearly twice the number of responses as cocoa, its closest contender. A fifty-nine-year-old Massachusetts woman writes, "My mother believed that almost any ill could be cured by 'sitting a spell, having a cup of tea and a goodie, if available, and a chat.' This seemed to work most of the time. I still use this method, even if the chat turns out to be with myself. It has become a . . . time for meditational thought." A New Jersey sales representative writes, "Sharing a cup of tea in the afternoon or in the evening is a comfort and a form of relaxation. Having a homemade treat with that cup of tea adds to the moment." Baked goods and tea, thus, appear to make the ideal comfort food and drink combination.

Concerns about health dampen some women's enthusiasm for talking about food and drink as comfort, since many named comfort foods—pot roast, meatloaf, spaghetti, and rice pudding, for example—are high in fat or have a heavier meat content than they consider safe or desirable. Still, many eat the food if Mother cooks it. Hamburger dishes, high in the named comfort foods, offer an example. A dish called hamburger gravy, known in my household as hamburger Stroganoff, came up as comfort food in one interview. Anne C., assembled with her two sisters and mother in that interview, recalled hamburger gravy and other hamburger dishes. "When I came home from college, the big treat was to go out for dinner, but all I wanted to do was stay home and have meatloaf or porcupine meatballs." Anne's sister Barbara C. remarked later in that interview, "If Mom were to have us over for meatloaf, we'd all be very happy." No one disagreed.

Kate L. thinks of her mother's hamburger hot dish as being comfort food, but Kate is now vegetarian, so it is no longer acceptable in her diet the way her mother (and her father's mother before her mother) prepared it. She shows with this recipe how she manages to continue to enjoy her childhood comfort food in new circumstances. Her husband Chris transformed the dish into a vegetarian dish.

## Old Style Faux Hamburger Hotdish
Chris Beatty/Kate Lynch
Mary Martin
Ethel Johnson Lynch

Kate's note: Add extra oil as needed while browning meat substitute. Add extra soy sauce with veggies for color and flavor.

1 large onion, chopped

1 package (2 cups) frozen corn

1 package (2 cups) frozen peas

6 small new potatoes, boiled and quartered

1 cup cooked brown or white rice

1 package meatless "Gimme Lean" (made by lite life) textured soy protein

3 cloves garlic, minced

3 tablespoons olive oil

¼ cup tamari soy sauce

salt and pepper to taste

1. In large skillet, brown onions in olive oil. Add meat substitute, garlic and soy sauce and brown, stirring occasionally.

2. Add rice and veggies and sauté for about 10 minutes.

Though the term *comfort food* has meaning and calls forth examples from most women, some react negatively, or with indifference, to the idea of comfort food. "I don't eat comfort foods when I need comfort" is the response a twenty-three-year-old New Jersey woman gave, for example, to the invitation to list comfort foods. No doubt some objections to comfort food come from knowledge about inappropriate uses of food, such as attempting to fill inner emptiness or dull painful feelings by eating, or substituting feeding for other forms of attention. Some women reflect their mothers' uses of food to these ends in reflecting on "the worst thing" about their food connection with their mothers. A seventy-five-year-old California homemaker writes poignantly, "She could not express her love except by overfeeding us. Food was overemphasized. I wish she could have bought canned vegetables from the store and lavished the interest she had for her garden on her children, instead of the garden. We needed her attention more than the food she produced."

Another woman, a forty-four-year-old office manager, shows how well-intentioned uses of food can degenerate into eating problems:

My mother could not afford to buy many new "material things" for us, because she raised seven children by herself after our father died. But she always told us she would never let us go hungry. . . . Thus, she overcompensated with food . . . and we used it to appease our emotions, leading to weight problems for a majority of us children. My mother, on the other hand, was very petite—she gave, we took!

A twenty-seven-year old-native of Germany writes that her mother used food and sweets as an antidepressant. Curiously, she views this as both the worst *and* the best connection she has with her mother!

These daughters feel, on the one hand, the lack of needed attention and, on the other, the physical consequences of too much nurturing through food. Perhaps because of questionable uses of food, even women who clearly have special feeling for certain foods decline to name them as comfort food. When one young woman went abroad to study for six weeks, she took along macaroni and cheese, a favorite of youngsters and a commonly named comfort food of adults. She does not view macaroni and cheese as comfort food, however. An older woman's response to an interview question about comfort food reveals her association: "No, we don't suffer from depression in our family." Later in the interview, however, she named custard as a comfort food.

Whatever problems some women have with comfort food, it is a source of pleasure to many. Seventy-one percent of women responding to the survey wrote in comfort food examples, and some wrote more than five, the number of blanks provided. The mother's part in providing comfort foods for children apparently seems to have an effect. Positive memories of Mother and food during childhood correlate highly with a mother's having prepared her daughter's named comfort foods.

## CELEBRATION FOOD

While daughters remember their mothers' offering food for illness and restoration, at other times the focus is on celebration. Anthropologists remind us that, in most societies, food and drink are used to celebrate "milestones of passages from one stage to another in the biological and social development of the individual." A birthday is such an occasion. Or when mother and daughter are reunited after the daughter has been away at college or comes to visit from her adult home, far from Mother. Food often figures prominently in these situations.

In my interview with Ruth and her daughters, the daughters spoke of how as children they got to pick their favorite meal for their birthday dinner. Survey respondents have similar memories. A twenty-six-year-old accountant writes that her mother makes a cake and the favorite dinner and bread of the fêted family member. A twenty-two-year-old Michigan woman had virtually the same experience, adding that her mother spends all day preparing such a birthday dinner, which always includes a homemade cake. Though she has long since left the family home, a Louisiana home-maker writes that her mother still provides her birthday cake.

Mothers put a lot of energy into creating these meals and special treats. Many do so after working all day. Judy Green Hergstriet refers in a letter to her daughter to "the nights you bake all night to give [your children] happy memories." But the attention can be important to daughters; they remember how special it made them feel.

A daughter's return home after a period away offers another occasion for celebrating with food. When my mother was still liv-ing and I visited her, I could always count on good things to eat. Especially vivid memories are the tastes of summer preserved in her frozen peaches and strawberries. Until she was unable to do so, she bought these beautiful fruits at peak goodness, preparing and freezing them for use in other seasons. She always offered them as dessert at a welcoming meal for me. Mothers (and sur-rogate mothers) often welcome daughters home with food. Fifty-nine percent of women say that when they get together with Mother, she prepares their special foods. As one food writer puts it, " 'What would you like to eat?' is the universal expression of love."

In my case, separation from my mother was due to our living in different parts of the country. This was also true for a psychi-atrist of my generation who grew up "next door" in Alabama, then moved north as I did. She writes, "I started to appreciate my mother's meals more especially when I was in situations when that type of food wasn't available. So coming home and eating Mama's cooking was increasingly important . . . through the years." Sarah Breathnach writes in *Simple Abundance* of how im-portant it was to her as well:

Whenever I've gone home to visit my parents, over the last twenty-five years, the first and last meal my mother has always prepared for me is my favorite: soup beans, a tangible time transporter to her old Kentucky home and mine. Soup beans are pinto beans that have simmered slowly for hours, until they create their own soup. Ladle soup beans over mashed potatoes. Serve with coleslaw, hot cornbread slathered with real butter, and an ice-cold beer.

I enjoyed a similar meal—of pinto beans, cornbread, coleslaw and buttermilk—many times at my mother's table and understand fully Breathnach's delight in this favorite meal.

Mothers may offer welcoming treats for separations as short as the school day. Joan Watts told a newspaper's food writer that her mother baked an after-school treat for her and her brother of a large glass bowl of custard. They stood in front of the refrigerator with two spoons and enjoyed it. Her mother died the year before she offered this memory. Now, when she misses her mother and feels sad, she makes the custard for her dad and herself. These little treats were no small thing for such women as a fifty-year-old New Jerseyite:

Because of her cooking and her comforting ways, my mother made a real home for us. When I remembered how I looked forward to homemade cakes or cookies when I came home from school, I wanted to create those same feelings of "it's great to be home" for my children. So what I am as a mother and a wife in terms of cooking, I owe to my mother.

Katie Cannon's idea as an adult of a "real" vacation is one where her mother feeds her. When her mother asks her what she wants for lunch, she hears it as an invitation to luxury. Sara Lawrence-Lightfoot writes of how, while she was working with her mother on a book about her mother's life, they kept a clear boundary between the necessary interviews and their family life. Her mother anticipated her visits with "special feasts," laid on a set table, following a sung grace. Jacqueline's mother always marked her visits home from college with a full breakfast in bed. Of that, Jacqueline says, "I will never forget." Carol's mother cooked spaghetti and meatballs for her when she came home from college. Anne W. served lasagna, a family favorite, when her daughter Jenny returned home from a time away, while Anne's own mother always prepared a roast for her homecomings.

Sometimes the separations involve troubling or otherwise stressful times. Marjorie Myers Douglas writes of being pampered by her mother with meals on trays and long conversations during her recovery from the birth of her youngest child. In her autobiographical *Gather Together in My Name*, Maya Angelou writes how "Momma," the grandmother who virtually raised her in her birth mother's absence, cooked for her when she returned to Stamps,

**FOR BETTER OR FOR WORSE by Lynn Johnston**

©UFS. Reprinted by permission.

Arkansas. Home from San Francisco, "the never-could-have-happened land," with all the pain of being left alone, with a baby, with no source of support, Maya would hear, "Sister, I made you a little something to eat." And Momma "bent to pull cakes from the wood-burning stove and arrange the familiar food on well-known plates, eras[ing] my control and the tears slipped out."

These examples suggest how food serves as a way for a mother to support her daughter. Whether commemorating her day of birth, or welcoming her home after a separation, special food serves as a symbol of celebration and a tangible way of caring.

## GIFTS OF FOOD

As if to insure that daughters at a distance are properly nourished and supplied with treats, mothers give gifts of food as well. Crystal Eastman, cofounder of the American Civil Liberties Union, wrote to her mother Annis Ford Eastman in 1907, the year she was admitted to the New York bar, about the cake her mother had sent. "The cake was in time for my dessert, and I think it is the best you ever made. Oh, you will never know just what it meant to me to have it come today! I have been feeling lately somewhat lost and stranded, as if I couldn't tell where or with what people I belonged.... And suddenly I knew that I belong to you. My lonely spirit was comforted; the world no longer seemed an empty place."

I remember what fun it was in college when someone's mother sent a box of treats. In our dormitory (all-women, of course, in those days), we shared these gifts of food with one another. A New Mexico woman remembers her own mother's sending her food when she was in college: "When I went away to college in Kansas City (my mom was in St. Louis), she would send me chocolate tortes from Swiss Colony for my birthday. One year she sent a ham for Easter."

Women living far from their national home receive special gifts of food from their mothers as well. In the gathering where the idea for this book first arose, a woman from India spoke of how her mother sent her pickles from home so that she would have "the right food." Later, I mentioned this to Martha K., also of Indian background but a native of Kenya. She nodded vigorously, and said, "Yes, now I do that for a niece who lives in Venice!" Martha, who lives in Minnesota, has advised her niece that pickles such as the ones she makes and sends are available commercially, but the niece assures her that the pickles she sends are *far* superior to the ones on the market.

In letters between Mira, an India-born woman who studied at the University of California-Berkeley in the mid-twentieth century, and her mother, Mira's mother displays this concern of mothers for her daughter's nutrition and "proper" eating. She writes, "I know you would laugh, but do take a glass of milk every night before going to bed, please." (She was surprised and puzzled to hear that Americans drink only cold milk.) Mira reports from America that "... food here is really tasteless. I miss your cooking and grandma's mango pickle and Choto mashi's special spinach...." Not long thereafter, her mother writes, asking, "Have you received the parcel I sent...? I put some pickles and other 'goodies' together.... I did not want to let your baba know about this. You know how much fuss he makes over food parcels. He always gives me big lectures that food in America is a thousand times better and more nutritious. As if that is enough!" Mira responds (even though, at this point, she is feeling suffocated by her mother's concern), "The pickles! Even the idea makes my mouth water!"

When I visited my mother in my adult years, she always sent me home with jars of pickles and other treats. Now, my stepfather's lovely and generous wife sometimes does that. The pear preserves she gave me one year were eyed greedily by a friend I visited on my way back home. ("Are those *pear preserves*???") My "othermothers" have also given me gifts of food. Virginia Black, my "fairy godmother," sent me boxes of shelled pecans from her trees in Hazlehurst, Mississippi, before she became unable to shell the nuts. And a beloved cousin of my mother's generation now gives me pecans to take home when I visit—a precious gift from my native South.

Marlyn, who lives on a hobby farm, said during her interview that, when they come to visit, she gives her daughters "salsa, jam—whatever they want. I tell them to go to the basement [where home-processed foods are kept] and help themselves." Barbara S., interviewed with her mother at the family lake home, remarked, "When we leave up here it will be with several jars of rhubarb jam." Jeanne C. told me that she always got some of the fifty jars of refrigerator jam her late mother made each year. A 41-year-old writes of her mother, "She is very generous. . . . She never lets me leave her house empty-handed and brings top quality frozen steaks and other treats when she comes to visit."

Thirty-six percent of women responding to the survey report their mothers send them food items, and 65 percent report receiving food from their mothers during visits. Many mothers never lose their desire to treat their daughters and to nurture them. These simple tokens of food are one way of fulfilling that desire.

## FOOD AND NURTURING MOTHER LOVE

The concern Mira's mother expresses for her daughter's nutrition in the letter from India quoted earlier, and her suggestion that nutrition is "not enough," points up a theme popping up continuously—that of food as nurture. While the notion of food as merely fuel crops up occasionally, most women invest food and feeding with far more than utilitarian meaning. The foregoing discussion of special uses of food shows how tied to caring and concern food is. And that commingling begins very early in a woman's life.

Nourishment begins upon conception, of course. A blessing for breast feeding from an eighteenth-century Hebrew women's liturgy includes the supplication, "[P]rovide for your gentle creation—plenty of milk, as much as she needs." Mothers worry about their daughters' getting enough food. The Darden sisters were fortunate as children. Their mother loved feeding them. "We were poor eaters, so she had to be creative with food, and she was. Surprises, sherbets, soups and basics—oh, what lovely treats we remember from Ms. Mamie Jean!" (The Dardens' use of the word *lovely* is particularly apt here.)

The late food writer M.F.K. Fisher suggests that "our three basic needs, for food and security and love, are so mixed and mingled and entwined that we cannot straightly think of one without the others. So it happens," she goes on, "that when I write of hunger, I am really writing about love and the hunger for it, and warmth and the love of it and the hunger for it . . . and then with warmth and richness and fine reality of hunger satisfied . . . and it is all one."

And women recognize the close connection of food and love. A forty-four-year-old New Mexico supervisor writes of her mother, "[Food] was her way of giving love, and I enjoyed receiving that love." Catherine, whose mother was a Nebraskan, spoke of food as nurture in one of the early focus groups I conducted. She gave an example. "Everybody always wanted to have the holidays at our house because my mother was such a wonderful cook. . . . It was her way of nurturing people. In the Upper Midwest, where people are less demonstrative, they do a lot of nurturing with food." Other women with Midwestern mothers agree:

- My mother's way of pleasing people and showing love is by cooking their favorite foods. There's a joke in our house: if you don't really like the food, don't say you do, or don't take a second helping, because you will be served that food every time you visit! My mother was never one for hugs and kisses, but food was and is a way she could show love. (Fifty-year-old editor)

- Making sure her family had enough good food to eat was a serious responsibility to my mother. It was an important part of her caring for and about us. When there wasn't enough money for extras, Mom always made sure we were well fed. She even prayed for food for us once, and a man stopped in with a deer roast. The satisfaction of having my family fed well (when they were home) is an offshoot of my childhood feelings of being taken care of. (Fifty-one-year-old sales administrator)

- My mother loves to cook for occasions and will make a dish [for a family meal] even if she isn't up to going—so the others can enjoy it. (Forty-three-year-old communications professional)

Ruth's daughters are all grown now and living independently. A woman devoted both to her adult daughters and the notion that wholesome food is essential to a good life, Ruth continues to nurture them, both by encouraging them to provide good food for themselves and by having them for meals. When I spoke with these women, Ellen said, "I started law school last week. [Mother] said, 'You need to eat well. It'll make you feel better, and it'll help your brain. You can come here for dinner.'" (Her mother lives near the law school.)

Feeding their children is truly a struggle for some women. Many manage to do it with little money, and some with more than ordinary results. One of the most poignant stories I ran across in my research for this book recounts the origin of the term *bosom biscuit*. It grew out of one African American woman's practice of bringing home for the children, in her ample bosom, buttered biscuits taken from the Virginia "big house" where she worked. "Sometimes," according to a grandchild, "these warm, buttered bosom biscuits were all the family had to eat." Grandma Mattie Flippin's husband had died, leaving her to support her extended family alone. According to a study of African American intergenerational communication, the term *bosom biscuit* thereafter came to signify nourishment for the "affective, cognitive, and spiritual" self as well as for the body. "Life is empty without your bosom biscuit. It's your food, it's the food that you got from your mother in your mind. It's what makes you continue. It nurtures you. It keeps you going, and if you don't have it anymore you are starving. You are talking about spiritual food."

African American women in particular tend to celebrate food and its connection with nurturing mother love. This theme is a focus in Akasha (Gloria) Hull's poetry. "The Taste of Mother Love" weaves the theme with others already discussed, such as learning to cook and the place of the kitchen in mother-daughter communication.

### The Taste of Mother Love

i. Dialogue: A Question and an Answer
Q. How come my food don't taste like yours?
A. That's the mother love in it, honey.
ii. The Fact
Make no mistake about it:
Mother love has taste.

That's what
>  seasons the beans
>  and salts the roast
>  and makes the cabbage taste good
>  (even when they're just cooked in bacon grease).

It's what
>  you yearn for on separated holidays
>  rush back to on vacations
>  and what makes you fat
>  (when you stay there too long).

It's why
>  you beg for a bite off mama's plate
>  (right after you finish cleaning your own)
>  and why home for you will always be
>  your mother's yellow, broken-backed kitchen.

iii. Learning Experience
I sit in my mama's kitchen, watching her cook.

Did you brown the meat before you set it in the oven?
How much onion did you put in that dressing?

Do you use milk or water in your cornbread? any eggs?
And how many spoons of sugar did it take to make the
>  potatoes this sweet?

What made your stew go from thin to thick like that?
Sometimes mine never does, no matter how long and slow I
>  cook it.

My mother's a patient woman;
she cooks and answers,
sometimes even in measurements and minutes—
if I keep pinning her down.

Later, I stand in my own kitchen, trying to cook.
I do it just so, remembering and following exactly
>  everything mama said.

BUT THEN, MY FOOD JUST WON'T TASTE LIKE HERS.

That's why when anybody says
cooking is a science,
I know better.

Ever been served contentment in a laboratory?
And any fool can tell you:
Real mother love don't grow on trees.

> "The Taste of Mother Love"
> ©Akasha (Gloria) Hull.
> Used by permission.

In her poem "8–5-88," Hull returns to the theme of food as nurture, writing that "the oil and salt of many solid women hum through my veins," and ending

I know
today—for sure—
I am somebody's mother

These greens I'm cooking
can nourish you

> "8–5-88" ©Akasha (Gloria) Hull.
> Used by permission.

The element of mother love in food is very real for some daughters. One of the most moving scenes in Anzia Yezierska's compelling novel *Bread Givers* is that of the heroine's mother coming to her little apartment, where she is starving and freezing, having left the family home, very much against the family code, to attend college and make a life for herself. Earlier, the heroine wondered why it was "that Mother's simplest dishes, her plain potato soup, her gefülte fish, were so filling. And what was the matter with the cafeteria food that it left me hungrier after eating than before?" The mother brings herring she has pickled, along with a feather bed. "I felt that nothing on earth was as warm as Mother's love."

While the association of food with love is fundamentally positive for most women, it has its pitfalls for others. Sara Lawrence-Lightfoot, who writes with such feeling about her mother's nurturing care, notes nevertheless, "So much love was wrapped up in the dinner ritual that many years later—as I struggled to lose extra pounds—I had to unlearn the habit of experiencing food as the embodiment of family love." Other women mention how mothers' desire to feed can cause difficulty. First, it is a desire that dies hard for some. A forty-six-year-old Californian remarks of her mother, "She keeps trying to feed you when you're full or watching what you eat." Dusty Sklar recounts how her mother insists on making something for the two to eat, even while she is dying. "Next time I let you feed me." This need of mothers to feed adult children becomes a burden to the children and even to the mothers themselves.

Then there is the opposite problem, that of daughters' associating their mothers' sparse feeding with sparse love. Thus, "the worst thing" about her connection with her mother through food, a fifty-seven-year-old teacher writes, was "her lack of nurturing, symbolized by her rather Spartan approach to food." It is interesting, though, that another woman in the same generation, whose mother provided little by way of teaching and nurturing through food, drew a different meaning from the same experience: "I never equate food with love. Also I never learned to push food on guests because she never did. It was just there. Consequently I've never been overweight or on a diet."

However women negotiate the food-as-love dilemma, it is important to take seriously the feeling that goes into food. If a variety of observers are to be believed, its power is not to be ignored. Karen Franzmeier of St. Martin's Table, a popular Minneapolis gathering place, believes that "when you make something out of love, good energy goes into it." And some cooks are self-consciously aware of this power. When Ann Cooper studied women chefs, one remarked to her, "When I cook, there's actually something, a feeling, I put in there." Another said of women's approach to food that "it is all about love." On the other hand, in the words of an Italian proverb, "If you're mad, you're going to cook mad food."

Recent interest in matters spiritual has brought to light a good deal of ancient wisdom about the importance of who cooks and with what feeling. Catherine, a Sufi teacher, remarked in one of the focus groups, "Some spiritual traditions believe that what the cook feels . . . puts a sort of energy into the food that causes it to be nurturing or not nurturing." In Hindu thought, for example, food brought or prepared with loving thoughts "create[s] a harmonious, happy result" for the recipient. Conversely, "If the cook is irritated while cooking, if he or she is grumbling or sighing, if he or she is miserable, wretched—all that is prepared in the food that comes before you." Sufi healers therefore express concern about the amount of food prepared by both machines and disgruntled restaurant workers. "The mental vibrations of such people inevitably work their way into the food." Marion Cunningham, longtime cooking teacher and food writer, likewise voices her misgivings about the deleterious effects of consuming food prepared by strangers.

Besides food preparation, of course, there is the matter of under what principles and with what care food is produced. The delights are well known of eating wholesome food grown at home, or by family members, friends, or other growers whose growing practices are known. As concerns grow about effects of pesticides, growth hormones, and other agricultural practices on both people and the land, many seek sources of food grown in alternative ways.

The implications of adding yet more criteria for selecting what is served at the family table can be scary, though. A legitimate fear is that obtaining food grown and prepared with care will become yet another burden for already-overburdened parents—expecially mothers. For, as Joyce Walker notes, our society's expectation for women to be the primary nurturers is "subtle and deep," and that includes, typically, overseeing the family food supply. The legacy of the domestic science movement left many mothers nervous about their capacity to provide correct nutrition for their families, and the constantly shifting ground in health research has only added to their insecurity. "Never," according to historian of family life John Gillis, "have mothers been so burdened by motherhood." So there is a risk of adding to that burden with higher standards for food sources and preparation.

But I suggest that closer attention to what goes into the food we eat means not so much never having meals out, or meals prepared by others, but choosing food sources wisely. Choices are more numerous nowadays, due to consumer pressure on the market. Many restaurants now serve wholesome foods, carefully selected. The closest grocery store to my home, a truly no-frills establishment, now offers (and advertises with an artistic neon sign!) organically grown vegetables, free-range chicken, and other products formerly available only at our local whole foods coop. That coop's phenomenal success and expansion—it is the largest single store coop in the United States—did not escape the attention of the mainstream market. Its aisles are crowded with customers seeking both raw and table-ready foods brought to the checkout counter under a set of principles coop customers value. Growing interest in the quality of food and its preparation can only increase options.

While acknowledging the importance of the feeling that goes into food, some observers caution us not to go overboard with too elaborate forms of showing care through food. Economist Ruth Schwartz Cowan writes of the emotional load feeding the family carried in the middle of the twentieth century; among other things, its purpose was "to encourage feelings of family loyalty and affection." Add to this concerns of nutrition, scheduling, and the logistics of simply getting something into the house and on the table, and the job is already beyond many people's capacity. Anthropologist Mary Catherine Bateson believes "We might be better off if we would separate food as nourishment and pleasure from food as the currency of care that leaves so many women laboring long hours to prove affection in that semantic muddle called nurturance. The ideal is to find simple forms that can be elaborated for delight or turned into art rather than onerous obligations. But the giving and receiving of these simple material tokens of caring will be essential." She writes earlier that "we enact and strengthen our relationships by performing dozens of small practical rituals, setting the table, making coffee" and asserts there is real worth involved in housekeeping. Indeed, she suggests that "we must transform our attitude toward all productive work and toward the planet into expressions of homemaking, where we create and sustain the possibility of life." Her use of the words *small* and *simple* suggest directions for thinking in a healthy way about food and love—for all concerned.

That many mothers invest food offered to their daughters with feeling is clear from the voices of women heard in these pages. Daughters' readings of their mothers' approaches to feeding, whether too generous or too spare, suggest the fine line mothers toe. But my work with women indicates that what daughters tend to notice most is the caring mothers show for them and for others through their approaches to food. The food may not be great, or it may be quite simple, but, in the end, if caring is there, daughters can, and do, keep the food in proper perspective. Conversely, the food may be superb, and quite elaborate, but if the focus is on culinary show, rather than on the people for whom it is prepared, daughters feel disappointed.

After my first public talk on mothers' and daughters' connections through food, a woman in the audience approached me and said, "I have something to tell you. When I go to visit my mother, as I approach the door I smell pot roast, even if she's not cooking it!" Near the end of her study on food, Susan Allport muses on what she is doing when she stands at the stove, cooking the family dinner, in sight of her daughters. "By filling my daughters with memories of foods tasted and savored and enjoyed in the company of our family, perhaps I am giving them a reason to keep coming home. Perhaps I am laying out a sensory path to our door." She probably is. Banana Yoshimoto writes in her novel *Kitchen* that "much of one's life history is etched in the senses." The memory—in the senses—of Mother's care in the extraordinary—and ordinary—times of life can call forth smells, sights, and tastes stronger than mere reality.

# 6

# "The Presence of Many Women": Food as a Way of Ensuring Continuity across Generations of Women

The book *In Memory's Kitchen*, described in Chapter 2, reveals dramatically just how strong is the desire of women to hand on their culinary traditions to their daughters. It recounts the extraordinary story of women in unspeakable circumstances, working without resources to write down their cherished recipes so that future generations could enjoy, preserve, and carry them forward. When, a quarter of a century later, Mina Pächter's daughter Anny opened the cookbook her mother had compiled in Terezín and entrusted to a friend to give to her, she was overcome with emotion seeing her mother's handwriting. "After all those years, it was like her hand was reaching out to me from long ago." *In Memory's Kitchen* is one of the great mother-to-daughter transmissions, as well as an extraordinary tribute to human hope.

Naomi Lowinsky's word for "the experience of continuity among women" is *motherline*. In *Stories from the Motherline*, she writes that women sort through the historical, cultural, and generational differences "that would make strangers of us if we could not bridge them." In a variety of ways, food serves as a bridge to keep women across generations from being strangers.

This chapter explores how material objects, recipes, traditions, and stories related to food help us continue our connections with our mothers and other women in our families. Survey respondents report the following top five connections to other women in their families through food: grandmother (70 percent), sister (56 percent), aunt (56 percent), mother-in-law (44 percent), and sister-in-law (32 percent). Examples in this chapter concentrate on connections with Mother, and to a lesser extent, with Grandmother and the mother-in-law.

## MATERIAL OBJECTS

Continuity through food manifests itself in a number of ways. Women tell of the family significance of a cookie mold or other utensil. Marlyn displays such family artifacts on her kitchen wall; her daughter Lynn says that, because of that display, she and her mother "talk about food, how food used to be done." Jacqueline, for whom a coffee urn, "always ready for company," symbolized her mother's commitment to offering hospitality, features that urn prominently today in the foyer of her home. During our interview, in which she named a variety of serving pieces and sets given to her by her mother, she brought out proudly and lovingly her late mother's heavy cut-glass party trays, now used in her own entertaining. In an interview with National Public Radio's Noah Adams, Joyce Maynard spoke of "several secrets of life, including the art of baking a great pie," that she received from her late mother. Her mother "swore by Pyrex" and used her own mother's Pyrex pie plates, now passed down in turn to *her* daughter.

Currently, I have little from my mother's kitchen in my own, since her kitchen is still intact and in daily use. When that household breaks up, I will ask first for her cast iron skillets. These craggy pieces, now blackened with over half a century's cooking (Jeanne Teller Leeson calls her own four-generation collection "black magic"), hold memories of cornbread, fried chicken, creamed white corn, and innumerable other foods of my childhood. Perhaps one reason women wax eloquent about these pots is their durability. For as Malya Grath Willits writes of hers, inherited from her mother, even after decades of use "they have more life left in them than any set of gleaming Calphalon." Vertamae Grosvenor speaks in stronger language, attributing more than durability to cast iron cookware, by comparison with more modern types: "Can't no Teflon fry no fried chicken." Grosvenor, a writer known to National Public Radio listeners for her food commentaries and special features, advises her readers to throw out all but black cast iron pots to get the right "vibrations" when they cook.

It is often Grandmother's and other older female family members' kitchen equipment and service pieces that are treasured. I have beautiful old china and serving pieces from my maternal grandmother and—one of my prized possessions—exquisite pink damask napkins from my cousin Helen. Jeanne E. spoke of her attachment to baking equipment passed down to her from her grandmother, "dishtowels that Gram made, that she embroidered. It's so funny; in my mind, I need *this* bowl, and there's a *certain* wooden spoon, and then I have [Gram's] two towels, and that's what I use to cover the bowl. There's that ritual. . . . It's maniacal, but that's [what I believe] makes it turn out every time."

Sandra inherited from her elegant grandmother Nana eight artichoke plates, among other serving pieces. They are the size of dinner plates, superbly designed for the eating of this special vegetable, with compartments for the artichoke, the melted butter for dipping, and the spent leaves. In talking about her grandmother's legacy, Sandra commented, "My love of cooking and entertaining, and my wonderful food memories, all center around her. When we entertain, half of the table setting is from her. We say things like, 'Wouldn't Nana be pleased that we're making this? Wouldn't Nana be pleased we're doing that?' "

Barbara C. related that when her grandmother died, the family inherited a wooden bowl with a curved blade. It is apparently the perfect tool for chopping nuts. Barbara remembers being about ten years old at the time the bowl devolved to her household. "Mom let me use it." She has it now in her own kitchen. The paternal grandmother in that family contributed, among other things, a china set used *only* to serve hot chocolate. Other daughters spoke of butter churns, silver flatware, and serving pieces.

Alice Walker demonstrates beautifully in her essay "The Blue Bowl" just how precious such items of material culture can be in a family. Walker's mother, a woman who worked hard and had little, in a material sense, kept the blue bowl full for her children of "whatever was the most tasty thing on earth." She gave the bowl to the adult Alice easily when asked, her generosity a symbol for Walker of "what she herself had represented in my life." Walker considers the bowl "perhaps the most precious thing I own."

Many women in the survey sample have food-related possessions of their mothers; 40 percent have kitchen equipment (the
older the woman, of course, the more likely she is to have it), 46
percent have or expect to get table service items, 41 percent (especially young women) expect to receive such objects in the future, and 38 percent report being told stories by their mothers
about kitchen equipment and table service. These material objects
are important in families, and when the older generations' households or possessions are divided, family members' wishes and
expectations often necessitate a careful process to handle their
passing down. Issues around who gets such "non-title" family
property are seen to be important enough for the University of
Minnesota Extension Service to develop an educational packet and
video, *Who Gets Grandma's Yellow Pie Plate? Transferring Non-titled
Property.*

## RECIPES

As *In Memory's Kitchen* so vividly illustrates, another way of
continuing women's traditions around food in a family is through
passing along and preserving recipes, or particular ways of preparing food. Lael spoke over lunch of recipes her late mother
wrote out for her: "They're dirty; they have food stains on them.
But I want to see *her* handwriting when I look at those recipes."
Jeanne E. spoke to her mother in our interview, "Remember, you
used to make chicken soup? And you always put nutmeg in it. I
. . . can't make chicken soup without getting the nutmeg and putting a little shake in. . . ."

As this second example suggests, one of the most common ways
of continuing Mother's cooking is simply to prepare her "dishes,"
at least periodically. One woman renamed some recipes to incor-
porate her mother's name; now the family routinely refers to the
dishes by those names when she serves them. A home care agency
director in New Mexico writes of the importance of using her
mother's recipes. "When I cook one of her dishes for others, I feel
as though she is smiling down on me from heaven. I am extremely
proud that I can cook like she did."

One woman spoke of her grandmother's recipes. "She had a
wonderful shorthand. I have to be really careful when I'm reading. . . ." This grandmother's recipe book, a three-ring binder writ-

ten in pencil, has been partially transcribed by the interviewed granddaughter.

Although women remark that some recipes they have from women in their family are not the kinds of food they eat now (Anne W. offered "midnight chocolate cake" in her interview as an example of one such delicious, but forbidden, recipe), they recall the goodness of these recipes. And they enjoy meals based on Mother's recipes when they get together with other family members. Anne reports that she and her sister have meatloaf when she travels halfway across the continent to vacation at the family home in Massachusetts each year. "It is the closest we have to a family recipe because most members of the family still make it when they are in Goshen."

## Granny's Meatloaf
Anne Webb
Marie Maloney Smillie

1 pound ground chuck

1 cup dry bread dressing

1 egg

½ cup milk

½ teaspoon salt

1 teaspoon Worcestershire sauce

2 teaspoons ketchup

1 small onion, chopped

slices of bacon to cover meatloaf

Mix all ingredients, and shape into a loaf. Put in casserole dish. Top with slices of bacon. Bake uncovered 1 hour at 350 degrees.

Sometimes when mothers pass along preparation of their specialties, daughters can become quite adept at them. A Texas photographer tells such a story:

Mother taught me to bake kolache about sixteen years ago. In our town
we have an annual celebration for the Czech pastry. The Kolache Festival
has been held the second Saturday in September for fourteen years now.
I've won the championship several years. We entered together one year.
I took all the awards. When my husband asked my mother if she was
disappointed she didn't win, she answered with a tear in her eye, "No,"
but that she was proud she had passed a tradition on to one of her
children.

That daughter is now continuing this aspect of her family's motherline by teaching her niece (her mother's granddaughter) to bake
kolache.

As this woman's story demonstrates, passing along to daughters family recipes for special ethnic foods keeps those traditions
alive. Marie remembers the porcelain-top table in her childhood
kitchen. Her mother, Josephine, would put a mountain of flour in
the middle and break eggs into it. Thus began the making of ra-
violi, a process that became a tradition for the Brama women.
Once a year for the past six decades, they have gathered to make
the pasta, filling, and sauce. Until Josephine's death a few years
ago, it was a four-generation undertaking. The ritual takes all day
and ends in an extended family dinner. Besides being a lot of fun,
this tradition helps keep the Brama women in touch with their
Italian-American roots. In some families, food serves as the primary conduit for learning ethnic traditions. A thirty-four-year-old
Virginia woman treasured times with her mother during the holidays, when they made traditional Mexican food together. "This
was one of the few times she would share a part of her past and
culture with me."

When the *Star Tribune* asked readers in 1999 to send in recipes
for a Mother's Day feature, they received recipes supplemented
by reminiscences—of comforting after-school snacks, of tomato
pancakes served on washdays and, in all cases, of "the love that
is the most frequently found ingredient." One recipe, for creamy
peach pie, came with the story of a mother who brought a requested piece of the pie to the hospital bed of a twelve-year-old
daughter. The girl's emergency appendectomy had ruined her
perfect school attendance record and her opportunity to participate in her town's annual festival. Now, when she has the pie,
she remembers how her mother cheered her up with it.

Stories like this about recipes are precious in some families. Elizabeth R. noted in her interview, "Mom talks about recipes from growing up—the importance of them, where they come from, what they mean . . . It's special." Casey related her favorite recipe story from her mother: "When she was in bed and dying of cancer, [my grandmother] heard a recipe on the radio for cut-out cookies called Angel Cookies, and she wrote it down from memory the next day. She died about two weeks after that. Angel cookies have always been our holiday cookie recipe. They are very white and soft, cake-like. The original recipe called for lard for the shortening! They are wonderful, and I've never found a sugar cookie that comes near to Angel Cookies."

## Angel Cookies
Casey Higgins
Agnes Hefner Higgins
Christina Ascheman Hefner

Casey's note: I copied this from Mom's old cookbook. They are our traditional cut-out Christmas cookies. They are delicious! My sister Tracy makes them every year, substituting another fat for lard and glazing them with egg yolk. The cookies may be decorated with colored sugars or iced after baking.

Sift:

1½ cups sugar

4 cups flour

3 tablespoons baking powder

¼ teaspoon baking soda

Cut in:

⅔ cup lard (or other fat, if preferred), as in pie crust

Then add:

2 eggs, beaten

1 cup sweet milk

1 teaspoon vanilla

more flour if needed

Dough can be refrigerated at this point, but should not be cooled too much. Firmness must be right to roll out and cut with cookie cutters. Bake in preheated 350-degree oven 8 to 10 minutes on greased cookie sheet.

Preserving handed-down recipes can take a number of forms. Often, women keep their mother's recipes with other recipes. This has been my own way. Some women, though, make special attempts to preserve recipes from the women in their family. These attempts include getting help from relatives regarding a deceased mother's methods of cooking, making up collections of family recipes for wedding gifts for the younger generation, writing down Grandmother's verbal instructions, setting up a computerized family recipe data base, and developing family cookbooks. Nancy told me her sister gave her a gift of a collection of recipes written in her mother's hand—laminated for preservation. Later, she sent me a copy of a letter one of her sisters had written to another, enclosing other of their mother's recipes. The note was full of reminiscences, including this comment: "It's funny, but when I read the recipes, it feels like Mom is close by. I can still see her bustling around the [Westchester County farmhouse] kitchen, dumping mice turds out of baking pans and cupboards."

Twenty-nine percent of survey respondents report giving mother's recipes to other women in the family, and 33 percent of those who have daughters have passed along their own mother's recipes. Sixteen percent have made special collections of their mother's recipes. Mothers themselves sometimes help with the work of preserving their recipes, beyond writing them out. Some make recipe files *for* their daughters. One daughter writes that she had her mother write down her recipes in a notebook. "She loved doing it." A woman I met at a Nebraska conference on mothers, daughters, and grandmothers told me about preparing for each of her married children a collection of family recipes, handwriting them on cards and placing them in a small photo album. The children cherish these collections, and "the women now use them for their holidays and special days."

But, like Akasha Hull, some women say that, even though they try, replicating Mother's cooking is impossible, written instructions notwithstanding. The notion that Mother does it best crops up often. Elizabeth R., interviewed with her mother Mary G., remarked, "You can read a recipe, but your heart has to be in it for it to come out the right way." Forty-five percent of survey respondents agree: "It never tastes the same."

In spite of the difficulty many daughters have reproducing the taste of Mother's cooking by following directions, however, and in spite of changing cooking styles and preferences, they still want their mother's recipes. This is true even for women who do not particularly want to *cook* from the recipes. One food writer believes it is the emotional connection that we have with the food that makes the recipes precious. Of women surveyed, 85 percent report having some of their mother's recipes; having those recipes is important to 69 percent.

Due to their mother's sudden death, some women were unable to get them. One such woman writes that when she was 14 years old her mother had a massive hemorrhage, so she was never able to get the recipe for her prize-winning pancakes or her Italian sausage. Marcia too was shocked when her mother-in-law died unexpectedly. "She was healthy, and we thought she'd live into her nineties. Food was one of my main connections to her. She was an excellent cook and baker." Marcia missed getting many of the recipes she wanted and vowed shortly thereafter "to get my own mother's recipes and food stories *this summer*, when she returns from her winter travels." Missed opportunities prompt some women, like a Texas auditor, to advise others to be sure to get their mother's recipes "while they are still around. So many people I know say, 'I wish I had a recipe that my mom used to make. She is no longer living, and I can't remember how she made it. Boy! Was it good.' "

## COOKBOOKS

Carol Leach told a food writer that she decided to collect her mother's recipes into a cookbook when her phone bill escalated from calls to her mother to ask cooking questions. My friend Jean

B. showed a cookbook like Leach's to me. Barbara North, a North Dakota woman, sent Jean and other friends a New Year's gift of a copy of the cookbook she developed from her mother's recipes. ("Anyone who knew Vicky Giger knew she loved to bake and cook.") The accompanying letter said that she got the idea when one of her mother's great-nieces requested one of her recipes as a memento. Doing the cookbook was a way for North to remember her mother, who had died the previous April. In my reading, and in my conversations with women about their mothers, I have come across a number of family cookbooks. Some merit special attention.

Judy Goldfein gave me the gift of the family cookbook she wrote when I interviewed her with Natalie and Miriam, two of her three daughters. Judy told me, "When my mother died, my project then became to do a cookbook. I found it both therapeutic and a wonderful gift to everybody I gave it to. . . . I would encourage anybody to do it." The book begins with a dedication to Judy's mother and what I call "a list of gratitudes." Taking the form, "I am grateful for . . . ," the frontispiece bespeaks a spiritual approach to life. The book's contents encompass not only recipes (some from her mother, some not), but also stories, events, and people Judy cares about. In the introduction, Judy writes that she decided to do the cookbook "to accommodate both my daughters' needs for recipes and my need to think about my mother." She thought writing the cookbook would be a way to document her mother's life but found it was a way as well to document her *own* life. She found that the process stirred up all kinds of "memories and ideas."

Among the recipes Judy contributed for readers of this book is one for her mother's Passover cake. The annotation Judy's daughter Heidi wrote for it demonstrates the richness of the motherline in this family.

# Ruth's Passover Cake
Heidi Goldfein
Judy Berman Goldfein
Ruth Schwartz Berman

Heidi's note: Passover is the time of year that is filled with thoughts of my late grandmother "Bubbe Ruth." The second night is her *jahrzeit* . . . but it is this holiday's meals and food that brings her back to us. She didn't shy away from the challenge of cooking for the Seders. My mother Judy follows in her footsteps in that sense.

Bubbe Ruth seemed to have discovered the following Passover cake recipe. I'd like to be able to say she just concocted it one day while tooling around in the kitchen, but I'm sure that would be a romantic version and probably revisionist history. Although I don't know its origins, I do know that she made it for Passover every year. Hence, it became her recipe. It's among the best Passover cakes our family has ever eaten. She always served it with fresh strawberries, topped with Cool Whip. Don't be afraid of the ingredients. Bubbe Ruth wasn't. What's another egg here or there, right?

For 12 servings:

9 eggs

2 cups sugar

1 lemon, rind and juice

1 orange, rind and juice

1 cup Passover cake flour

1 teaspoon cinnamon

1 teaspoon ginger

¼ cup chopped nuts

1 dash salt

Beat the yolks with the sugar and add the juice. Beat the whites with the salt until stiff. Add the yolks to the whites.

Add spices, rinds and some nuts to the flour. Fold flour mixture into egg mixture. Add rest of nuts. Put mixture into a very clean ungreased tube pan. Bake at 325 degrees for 1 hour and 15 minutes. Cool before removing from pan.

A cookbook given to me by another participant illustrates a second such effort. The handsome cover of *At Martha's Table*, occasioned by the subject's eightieth birthday, pictures Martha Stadther standing by her dining table, about to place the floral centerpiece. The table is laid with candles and special holiday china. Behind her, lined up on the bookcase, stand family photographs. Stadther's biography, complete with photographs, opens the book. Nearly one hundred pages of recipes follow, accented by sidebars with comments from the family about the recipes and Mother's cooking ("I'll bet we were the only kids from Olivia [Minnesota] who had a mother who was a gourmet cook").

Just how important family cookbooks can be to those who cook from them is illustrated by Anne C.'s story of a desperate aunt's telephone call: The dog had urinated on her family cookbook, and it had to be thrown out; she needed the porcupine meatball recipe for a dinner.

Most family cookbooks are privately printed. Some, however, make it to the trade book market. A particularly delightful example of such a book is *Spoonbread and Strawberry Wine: Recipes and Reminiscences of a Family*. Norma Jean and Carole Darden begin their book "We are sisters who love to cook, especially together." More than a collection of recipes, the book includes memories, family history, and stories the recipes invoke. The Darden sisters write of "the magical instincts" that guided the women in their family, who "rarely measured or even tasted" what they were cooking, of their mother, who "used to tell us that good food inspires good thoughts, good talk, and an atmosphere of happiness."

## OTHER TRADITIONS

Of course many women do not cook from recipes. Marvalene Hughes writes that many African American women of her mother's generation continued to carry ways of preparing food in their heads and passed them down through oral tradition, that method having been necessary during slavery's enforced illiteracy. "My mother never cooked from recipes" is the comment of a thirty-four-year-old who grew up in Iowa. Nor did mine, usually. I found when I went through her recipes that most of them were for desserts. This puzzled me greatly until I realized that Mama's regular cooking at home (as opposed to at work, where she supervised cooking in quantity) depended very little on recipes. It was only special, less frequently cooked items—desserts, in fact—that required her to follow written instructions. But this was not peculiar to Mama, apparently. Southern food chronicler John Egerton writes that it is "not at all unusual to find sacrifices to the legendary Southern sweet tooth taking up at least half the pages in a cookbook."

Catherine Manton writes about the downside of women cooking from recipes. She believes they can undermine the cook's confidence and creativity and that the advent of domestic science, in fact, interrupted the passing down of family traditions in cooking—a hazard Hughes says African American women have avoided by rejecting "scientific progress in food," relying instead on "taste, smell, sight, touch, and . . . soulful intuition." But women who have little experience cooking, and little opportunity to get that experience easily, often need recipes. Indeed, as noted in Chapter 4, even cooking from recipes requires some experience. Philosopher Lisa Heldke remarks, for example, that "the way you treat recipes often reflects your degree of skill and confidence as a cook, your spirit of adventure, your knack for imagining what foods might taste good together." So both written instructions *and* experience appear to be necessary, and some daughters who have neither express regret that they cannot continue their mother's, and other family women's, cooking traditions. A Maine manager remarks, "I wish that I had paid more attention to how [my mother and my grandmother] cooked when I lived at home. They made a lot of ethnic foods that have no written recipes, so we can't recreate the food."

But even in cases where Mother's recipes are not written or her "dishes" preserved in other ways, women may carry forward certain traditions, preparation, and service techniques. A baking specialty, for example, came up in several participants' contributions. In one family, baking is the thread of continuity, with each woman manifesting the tradition in an individual way. Kathleen, a seventy-eight-year-old interviewed with her daughter Jeanne E., recalled how her grandmother baked on the farm. Her rye bread and kolaches are legendary: She made kolaches *every day* for the next day's breakfast. Kathleen herself did not carry forward the baking of loaves of bread but did bake yeast rolls and kolaches. Jeanne, however, bakes all the bread her family consumes, including loaves, and involves her daughters Kate and Jali in the process. Kolaches are a special treat now; no one makes them every day!

A farm background is not required for such family traditions. Urban families have them as well. In her interview with her daughter Elizabeth R., Mary G. related her childhood in a three-generation household in the heart of the city. Her grandmother baked for the family and was wont to say, "Get out of the kitchen; this is baking day." Mary remembers twenty-five-pound bags of flour, special breads. A particularly vivid memory is the baking of loaves of Easter bread in the shape of a rabbit. "My grandmother's brother was an artist. He drew a picture, and Grandmother took it to a tinsmith and had him make large cutters. Grandmother died with that recipe in her head. Mother tried to replicate it. Friends expected their rabbit! I still have the tins." Mary still makes "bunnies," but with another recipe.

Sara Lawrence Lightfoot shows how some women adopt their mothers' ways of food service as well as their recipes. In a loving biography of her extraordinary mother, Margaret Lawrence, a woman who overcame huge barriers of race and sex to become a psychoanalyst early in the twentieth century, she relates how, as an adult, she identified increasingly with her mother until "in my mid-thirties . . . the identification . . . was complete." Among examples she gives of her identification with her mother are that she "now became a baker of 'Maggie Bread,' the hearty whole wheat variety, with my own embellishment of raisins. . . . Now I tried to put the pieces of my own busy life together, racing home to place bright napkins and candles on the dinner table. . . ." Jacqueline, too, mentioned the use of cloth napkins, adopted from her mother's practice, in our interview. "Those napkins were so special for [Mother's] guests to use . . . the softness to the face and everything. She was quite a hostess. She took delight in doing those kinds of things. And surprisingly, I find myself doing the same things."

One three-generation interview revealed how traditions of service change across generations. Beverly, who lays a beautiful table, recalled that her own grandmother had few presentation skills. But her mother, who raised her daughters alone with little money, "loved the right tablecloth. And when we lived in apartments [so small] you could hardly move, she had a Duncan Phyfe table that would seat seventeen. It took up the whole living room when we had Thanksgiving dinner. Of course, she didn't have good china and all that to go with it." Beverly's daughter Kevlyn also places strong emphasis on presentation. Economic circumstances may constrain the way women are able to lay a table, but the valuing of presentation leads women across generations to work for it in ways they can manage.

Like other ways of living, children learn to value presentation by observing it. Beverly's recollections demonstrate that the way food is served makes an impression on children. Jeanne E. spoke in her interview of the family table of her childhood, "the sunlight through the glass and the good glasses. We do that same thing here. It tickles me. . . . I have no doubt that my daughters will set tables and fuss over food and take the recipes. They are adding to [family tradition], but they are taking away the core of it." Earlier in the interview, she remarked that her children already have "a tremendous sense of ritual about having meals with people."

## STORIES

Writer Dorothy Allison has said that "food is more than sustenance; it is history." Women learn from their mothers family history and stories connected to food. A forty-year-old freelance illustrator writes that the best thing about her relationship with her mother through food was "her history, which was closely tied to it. I learned more about my maternal ancestors and family via food than in any other way." Another woman, a fifty-two-year-old human resources manager, writes of her mother, "The discussion of food triggers memories, which cause her to tell lots of family stories and history."

Some of my own mother's food stories seemed odd to me. She

told me, for example, how embarrassed she was as a child of the homemade bread in the bag lunches she took to school. Homemade bread for lunch sounded good to me! During her era, though, packaged sliced bread was a sign of prosperity, and her family's means were meager indeed. As it turns out, attributes of bread, as well as other foodstuffs, have signaled rank since ancient times.

Beverly told the story of how her mother's history on the family farm developed a quirk she continues to display half a century later—that of always encouraging diners at her table to eat more bread. As in many other families throughout the nineteenth and early twentieth centuries, the women in Esther Olson's family were integral parts of the farm operation. (See Chapter 8 for more on this topic.) One of their jobs was to provide enough food for the enormous appetites of the hands. Esther fed the threshing crew with one dollar a day. The grandmother brought meat and cream, and they used their own garden produce. At the table, Esther would say to the crew, "Have some bread; we've got plenty of bread." That embarrassed her daughter. "When I was older, I realized that bread was what was plentiful." But her mother *still* says this at the table.

Family stories about food are not limited to "days on the farm" or Depression horror stories. Nor are they all of women's culinary heroism. Stories mothers tell can imbue ordinary practices and material objects with more than ordinary meaning. A forty-two-year-old who grew up in Illinois writes that her mother related stories of "what she would eat at a particular time of year, on a particular holiday, or with particular relatives; how the wooden bowl for chopping cabbage got a crack; the special birthday cake plate; and of her mother's canning, baking, growing, stretching a little."

Food stories also provide good laughs. Some are about how mothers managed—or didn't—with limited cooking skill or interest. A twenty-nine-year-old Michigan woman, who says some of her best family stories are about food, offers one about how her mother "learned to make Jell-O to impress my dad." Another tells of "disastrous things done with Jell-O." (Jell-O comes in for its share of jokes.) Leslie Hale, who developed a family cookbook, writes of how her mother once "accidentally dredg[ed] sole in powdered sugar instead of flour." Helen spoke with amusement of her mother's approach to meals. A busy community activist, seamstress, and church worker, she was often away from home during the day. "Mother got dinner on the table thirty to forty-five minutes after my father came home. She would come in at maybe 4:30 from her activities, fly in the kitchen, and say to my sister Karen and me, 'Quick! Dust the house! Make my bed!' And when Dad got home, she would be cooking." Helen added that, in order to avoid having cooking impinge on her activities, her mother was always among the first to try new products designed to shorten meal preparation.

Bailey White, who has published quite a few of her late mother's antics in books and read not a few of them on National Public Radio, writes often of food. She tells of trips to Rosey's, "a raunchy juke joint" near their Georgia home, to dine on smoked mullet. White is apprehensive about the characters who frequent Rosey's, but "Mama doesn't notice. She just likes the mullet." Besides frequenting questionable venues for favorite meals, Mama's unorthodox behavior extended to obtaining meat in unusual places. In "Dead on the Road," White details her mother's favorite road kill meals. An "excellent and adventurous cook," she served a range of finds—doves, robins, quail, and turkey. She declined, however, to try armadillos—"too stupid to eat."

Funny stories about food often originate in holiday cooking. At Christmas one year, our friend Elizabeth presented my husband and me with a beautiful plum pudding. "One of our favorite family stories is that Mother, a lifelong teetotaler, embraced the flaming brandy [used to serve the plum pudding] after a physician friend told her the alcohol disappeared with the burning. Henceforth, she kept a bottle of brandy in the living room window seat that overlooked her rose garden." When Elizabeth gave me her recipe for this dessert, she wrote as well of its long history with the women of her motherline: "I copied the recipe from a postcard my mother (Elizabeth Clark Plankinton, 1890–1986) sent to me in 1952. It reads in part, 'History repeats itself. On November 18, 1916, my mother (Margaret Cowan Clark, 1849–1921) wrote this for me. It was brought from England by my father's mother (Elizabeth Nunns Clark, 1815–1889) and grandmother.' " Elizabeth's mother's suggestions for translating the old-fashioned recipe appear in parentheses; for "1 pound flour," for example, she wrote "(3½ cups flour)."

The making of fruitcake, rather than plum pudding, was my family tradition at Christmas. Of course, an entire book could be filled with jokes and stories about fruitcake, that much-denigrated foodstuff. But I loved my mother's fruitcake. For years after she was unable to make it and give it to me at Christmas, my mother-in-law Clare filled the gap. Now she, too, has ceased to bake fruitcake. For the last few years our friend Helen has given us fruitcakes made from her family recipe—gratefully received and greatly enjoyed. I learned recently of the shopping, preparation, labor and time it takes Helen to produce the fruitcakes she gives at Christmas. As she tells the story of making fruitcakes with her mother, Etna, and her grandmother, "Gommy," it is easy to understand her comment, "I don't know if anyone outside my family would ever want to spend the time to bake this. But it was a great holiday event for us. . . ." The women of Helen's family baked the cakes in October, then brandied them for two months before serving or giving. "Mom says that more than one year, she and Gommy got tipsy during the [fruit and nut] cutting-up process. Gommy was a regular wine-drinker, and it didn't show on her. But Mom can't take a drink without getting slightly loud and having a tendency to sing. Fruitcake-making was a bonding process for them. When my sister Karen and I began to help, fruitcake making was the essence of Christmas." Helen gave me the amazing recipe for this legendary family fruitcake. Near the end of the lengthy instructions appears the suggestion, "Hire someone to clean up."

Family stories come not only from the older to the younger generations; daughter-to-mother stories become part of the family story pool as well. Sometimes the stories recount childhood pranks related to food. One woman hated egg foo young as a child. She fooled her mother by loading such unwanted food into a large toy truck she brought to the table regularly. At a convenient time, she surreptitiously dumped it out the back door on her mother's bed of ivy ground cover. Ironically, the girl's mother and father made this feat easy by a family policy: any child who did not finish dinner was left at the table to do so while the rest of the family retired to the living room to say the rosary. When her mother learned, years later, about her daughter's disposal of the unwanted food items, she remarked, "I always *wondered* why the ivy did so well in that spot!"

I fooled my mother once. In spite of her openness to new foods; she was completely close-minded when it came to lamb, as are many of her generation. Her early-life experiences with lamb, or probably mutton, soured her on lamb forever. Not surprisingly, then, I had never tasted lamb when I struck out on my own after college. As I moved steadily northward, then westward, lamb began to be presented to me increasingly. By the time I was thirty, I was a confirmed lamb lover. We served it for special meals, ordered it in the Greek and Lebanese restaurants we frequented, and even bought entire lambs. When Mama came to visit one year, I took the risk of serving her lamb as *we* knew it, not telling her what it was. She loved it.

Writing on food bonds in families, Barbara Buchholz describes food as "an heirloom we bequeath to define the families we are part of." She suggests family food culture offers "a powerful legacy, [ensuring] immortality by linking past and future generations." Women have been the primary carriers of the food legacy. Cokie Roberts writes in *We Are Our Mothers' Daughters* of "the thread of continuity with women throughout the ages." As diverse as we are, she notes, similarities in our stories override the differences. The women contributing to this book attest to that truth. Their interest in the women of their motherline—their traditions of cooking and service—suggest that no matter how different our lives from those of our mothers, grandmothers, and other family women, we have a link to them. It is a link worthy of maintenance, through reflection and use.

In her challenge to honor especially the women who have gone before, Luce Giard writes, "As long as one of us preserves your nourishing knowledge, as long as the recipes of your tender patience are transmitted from hand to hand and from generation to generation, a fragmentary yet tenacious memory of your life itself will live on." At my mother's funeral, a woman approached me and introduced herself as a school lunchroom manager in the local school system. She had started to work in school lunchrooms as a kitchen worker under my mother's supervision. The woman knew nothing when she began. Mama's skill in managing food service and using food commodities effectively, and her creativity in enticing school children to eat what they needed but normally would not eat, were legendary. "Your mother taught me everything I know about food," she went on. "I owe her so much." When Mama's recipes were sorted, with her other effects, her quantity cooking recipes went to this woman, while the family recipes came to me. It makes me happy to think of her, and of others, who benefited from my mother's "nourishing knowledge."

Occasionally, a woman tells me that her mother makes light of the meaning she invests in what her mother and other women have done with food. In a memoir focussed on the kitchen, one writer tells of speaking appreciatively to her mother about how she "kept the flame alive." Her mother protested, "I wasn't trying to keep a flame alive. . . . You children had to eat something and I did what I knew how."

*Nevertheless*, I say. *Nevertheless*.

# 7

# *"What Life Requires":*
# *Messages about Life*
# *through Food*

When journalist Reagan Walker became a food writer, she reflected on what she gained, "beyond kitchen techniques and a collection of recipes," from her mother, who has worked variously as waitress, caterer, restaurant owner, and culinary mystery writer. Among her lessons were that "preparing a feast for friends and family is a way of loving. And like loving, sometimes it's hard work. Often it requires resourcefulness and begs for creativity. Occasionally, there are disappointments." Walker's lessons, like the lessons many women learned by watching their mother's approach to food, extend beyond the kitchen and table. They apply to other life domains as well.

Mothers do not necessarily teach these life lessons directly. Daughters learn them from messages mothers send, whether explicit or implicit. At the meals I hosted in my early efforts to explore mothers' and daughters' connections through food, women brought up these messages spontaneously. After those exploratory sessions, I pursued with other women the idea of messages about life through food. The body of messages collected range from common aphorisms ("A watched pot never boils"), to more originally stated bits of wisdom ("Persistence wins out over talent and genius"), to the cleverly subtle ("Some things just will not mesh together; they will always clash. The stronger 'flavor' will over-power the rest").

Colleen recalled the way her mother communicated to her *the importance of being prepared*. "I can remember her talking with me about how to organize my activities. She said when I married, 'You just need to know how to cook two good dishes for com-pany' . . . and we went home and made eight pies that day so I could get the hang of pie dough. . . . It's not that I hadn't cooked well enough, it's that it was time to *be ready*. She always wanted me to be ready." Other women since have echoed Colleen's mes-sage from her mother about planning and organization. In an in-terview with her mother, for example, Jenny remarked, "If you can get a meal on the table at 6:30, probably the rest of your day and life are going to be somewhat organized." And Anne C. spoke of how, when she went to graduate school in Toronto, her mother advised her to plan ahead by stocking up on inexpensive, nutri-tious food to take along: "Buy a case of white tuna packed in water when it goes on sale."

Interview participants generally answered easily when I asked what messages they learned observing their mothers' approach to food. A couple of women spoke of learning to take risks; their adventurous mothers, for example, defied the common practice of cooking for dinner guests only the tried and perfected. (A survey respondent calls this the message of "fearlessness.") Another talked about how food occasioned learning about fairness and about sharing; if her mother placed a bowl of peaches on the table, everyone in the family knew that each member would have at least one of those peaches. (She learned later in life that other families operated differently.)

While nearly all interview participants offered life messages readily, responses were proportionately fewer from survey re-spondents, who must reflect on the question and compose an an-swer in writing. Still, 40 percent offered over 300 messages, and some were delightful, such as that of the New Mexico service agency director who conveys her mother's message thus: "Do it with love, do it with style, do it from scratch."

This chapter includes messages gleaned from women's reflec-tions, offered in group discussions, interviews, surveys, published material, and individual conversation, on what they "hear," or "heard," through their mothers' approach to food. Following examination of the four top messages—conserve resources, make do with what you have, share/offer hospitality, and offer abundance—are other common messages and, finally, some problematic messages.

## CONSERVE RESOURCES

By far the most common message, representing over a quarter of all messages offered, is to conserve resources, or avoid waste. Survey respondents often report this message with a terse "Waste not, want not." "Use it all—find a use for it rather than throwing it away" is the message a Louisiana attorney got. A twenty-seven-year-old medical secretary recounts where she thought this message came from: "My mother helped her grandmother, who was blind, do *all* her household chores and cooking, from the time she was six years old until she was seventeen years old. She learned how to 'use everything and waste nothing'—pioneer recycling."

Survey respondents in their fifties demonstrate the kinds of messages middle-aged women received in the kitchen relative to conserving resources. Some give specific examples to show how one can use what is often thrown away. One mentions drying celery leaves to use in soup. "The idea was not to waste *anything*, not even flour that had weevils in it," writes a New York librarian. "They're extra protein." (Luckily, this woman's mother did not rear children during the "Ew, gross!" era.) An Avon representative from Texas shows how closely tied are the messages of conservation and creativity: "You can always use leftovers in a creative way the second day after cooking."

Even food that some consider beyond use may be useful. Bertie's recipe using stale cheese demonstrates how women in her family tried to avoid waste.

## Biscuits Made with Stale Cheese

Bertie Wells
Lucille Sherry Dorr
Artie Sherry

Bertie's note: This recipe is written on the end paper of a 1927 *Good Housekeeping's Book of Good Meals*. Delicious served with salad.

For 48 tiny biscuits:

2 cups flour

2 heaping teaspoons baking powder

½ cup shortening

1½ cups grated stale cheese

Mix flour and baking powder. Cut shortening into flour mixture until crumbs are pea-size, as for piecrust. Stir in cheese. Roll dough. Cut out biscuits with very small cutter. Prick tops lightly with a fork and bake in a 400-degree oven.

Many mothers feel strongly about not wasting, and they communicate this to their daughters. Barbara S., interviewed with her mother Winn, elaborated: "[There are] messages about waste and abundance. On the one hand, abundance and sufficiency are appropriate, and everyone deserves that. On the other hand, to waste what you have is not just stupid; it's really quite immoral." Winn agreed that she "cannot waste." She went on, "I'll use my mind in any way possible to disguise [leftover food] and give it to my husband another time—because he doesn't like leftover food." And, indeed, using the mind is required. It takes good management from the start, to plan how much to cook in the first place to avoid excessive leftovers, then ingenuity to figure out how to use odd bits of food that *are* left over, especially if they are to be disguised!

Some daughters find their mothers' leftovers far more appealing than their own. As Lynn put it, "Nobody's leftovers are as good as [Mother's], though. I throw away leftovers at my own house, but I'll go to her house and look and see what's left over." Another daughter, Elizabeth R., recalled of her mother, "Daily meals were always good and seemed well-prepared—even leftovers. She has that knack. I don't think I have it yet. Hopefully, it'll come."

Generally, middle-aged mothers are more concerned than their daughters are about not wasting food. But some younger women feel just as strongly about waste. One mother of young daughters, interviewed with her own seventy-eight-year-old mother, re-marked, "I'll never not have a twinge when they leave things on their plate. That's not acceptable. It's in front of you, and it's your opportunity. . . . I have a Depression-era mentality about waste that is a direct line from Mom." Her mother replied that, during the Depression, "[Money] *wasn't there*. Those were hard times. You had, you saved. . . . You still enjoyed life if you didn't have it. Nobody else had it either! My generation is very much that way." "But I am, too," the daughter replied, "And I don't *have* to be." Earlier, the mother had talked about using everything from slaughtered animals—kidneys, brains, sweetbreads, cracklings— on the Wisconsin farm where she grew up. This took me back to my own childhood in Georgia, where visits from my city home to "the country," as we called it, offered such treats as cracklings, and brains and eggs. Lillian Smith, another native Georgian of the generation before my own, writes of this practice of using all parts of the hog in a memoir of her childhood.

Many women mentioned the "Depression mentality" in con-nection with the message to conserve. One, for example, said, "Mom was a teenager when the Great Depression hit, and she never quite got over it." Some contemporary women speak of this approach to life disparagingly as "coming from scarcity." Coming from scarcity suggests there is not enough of what we need. It connotes fear and worry that can lead to extraordinary measures to ensure adequate resources. This stance can be a burden, espe-cially for older women with diminished energy to do the work associated with it. Some women describe in painful terms the strain on their mothers of managing food the way a conservation ethic requires. But, as noted earlier, some younger women live by this ethic as well. Increased emphasis on recycling has made the management of food and other consumer wastes easier. Many women now recycle or throw onto their compost piles what their mothers would have saved or felt guilty about throwing away. Compost piles and other ways of transforming waste into usable material both reduce garbage to be disposed of and offset some of the guilt generated by throwing away spoiled leftovers occasionally.

Living by a conservation ethic is in direct opposition to a throw-away culture and the waste it generates. It is an ethic I try to live by (I got it from my mother!) and one that I occasionally go overboard with. (My spouse fervently wishes I would throw out leftovers that sit in the refrigerator more than a couple of days.) How one *applies* the message to conserve can make all the difference. As a prompt to living responsibly, it is beneficial.

## MAKE DO WITH WHAT YOU HAVE

One of the most innovative people I ever knew once challenged me to think about the "what-ifs." At the time, a work group was meeting to solve some problems with limited resources, and some members of the group started brainstorming "what-if" scenarios. Later, in a review of the meeting with my boss (the innovative person), I expressed my scorn at such idle speculation. I thought I was being a realist by rejecting such nonsense. "What is, *is*," constituted my approach to life at that point. My boss moved swiftly to correct my negative judgment of such "dreaming," as I was wont to designate it. "Asking 'what if,' thinking about alternative ways of setting up and viewing the situation, can be highly productive," he said. He spoke as if he was sure. I paid attention because of my respect for him and his work and have since learned the wisdom of his words. Imagining the what-ifs encompasses both realism (we do not always have what we would like) *and* creativity (we can make something of what we *do* have). It helps in the kitchen as well as in the office.

Exploring the what-ifs relates directly to the second most common message about life through food, that of making do with what one has. It comes out of women's work with food, because we often do *not* have everything called for in a recipe, or at least in the amount needed. What if I substitute celery braised in broth for the artichoke hearts called for in this cold salad entrée? What if I take these couple of fish filets the two of us were going to broil for dinner and, instead, cook them with rice and vegetables to make enough for us *and* the friends who stopped by unexpectedly?

Women learned from their mothers both by word and deed how to make do. A Texas manager writes, for instance, "There's more than one way to do something; don't be afraid to experiment; follow instructions [the first time], then do it your own way." A Tennessee teacher remembers, "Even if there was very little money, [my mother] could make a tasty and satisfying meal— much better than anything we ate out!" "She is so skilled at making something out of little and being flexible with ingredients. If you don't have one thing, add something else instead," is the way a sixty-two-year-old Georgia homemaker described her mother's example. Women who live by this message, in short, know how to do something interesting—or at least sufficient—with what is available.

Colleen's mother had this capacity. "She was ready to cook in a minute. My dad owned a hardware store, and he would call and say, 'I have six people I'd like to bring home in fifteen minutes. Can you do it?' And she always said, 'Sure.'" My mother, too, was quite inventive in making something of what was available. She could present a tasty meal at a moment's notice without a trip to the grocery store. I have this capacity as well, apparently having absorbed it from her. By contrast, my spouse, who routinely prepares far more elaborate meals than I, is often at a loss to come up with something when he hasn't planned in advance and when all 'necessary' ingredients are not on the shelf. He often remarks on my ability to produce a meal from what appears to him to be nothing.

One woman commented in an interview on the usefulness of this message. "You [learn that you] make it up as you go along . . . that you can be inventive and vary and [be] creative and that that's not only allowable but it's what life requires in some ways. That's certainly part of the way I cook and try to live my life." Thus, in writing about women's lives, Mary Catherine Bateson compares the process of "composing" a life to improvisational cooking.

In her study of cooking in everyday life, Luce Giard writes, "Alimentary habits constitute a domain where tradition and innovation matter equally, where past and present are mixed to serve the needs of the hour, to furnish the joy of the moment, and to suit the circumstance." Innovation often happens in food preparation because of the need to improvise. Whatever they have, women who master the skills of improvisation learn to make something of it, and with it.

While many women learned to do this kind of cooking during the Depression, when many families had scarce resources, nowadays, many affluent women experience making do as a challenge to their management skills and creativity. For poor women, however, as sociologist Marjorie DeVault points out, making do, sometimes with extremely limited resources, remains a necessity. Marvalene Hughes explains how African American women manage and even triumph in scarcity: ". . . economics cannot control her soulful creativity in the preparation of foods. Consider some of the classic foods that are labeled soul food: pigs' feet, ham hocks, chitterlings, pigs' ears, hog jowl, tripe, cracklings, chicken backs, giblets, chicken wings, and oxtails. All of those were initially leftovers or 'throw-aways' given to Blacks who wanted to believe they were in a land of plenty. . . . The survival-oriented Black woman trusts her creative skills to 'make something out of nothing.' " African American women have often excelled using their creativity in the kitchen. Indeed, in cooking, "Everything is creating," according to celebrated African American chef Edna Lewis. As noted earlier, the message of making do with what one has relates closely to conserving. But using one's wits to manage what *is* as the basis for a new creation develops an added dimension.

## SHARE/OFFER HOSPITALITY

The daughter in Anzia Yezierska's novel *Bread Givers* reflects on the delight her mother took in entertaining: "[H]ow her face lit up whenever company came! How her eyes sparkled with friendliness as she served the glasses of tea, spread everything we had on the table, to show her hospitality." Other women observe this value in their mothers as well. Elizabeth S. remembers how her mother would say brightly, "We have to have a party!" The party meal, situated as it was on the Pacific coast, might include individual crab salads. If the preparation got frantic, she would invite the guests to help. "Mother was so much fun. She could laugh when things went wrong."

During interview sessions, many women spoke of their mother's hospitality. And of women surveyed, 83 percent agree that they value offering hospitality, while 81 percent agree that their mothers do or did. The third most common message from their mothers for these women is the importance of sharing and of offering hospitality.

The largesse of a hospitable approach is exemplified in the message of a New Mexico registered nurse's mother: "If *I* have a bean, then *you* have *half* a bean." Completing the section on household demographics in her survey (five people live in her household), this woman adds in the margin, "There are always extra people at my table—no less than six, often twelve." A Maryland marketing professional heard this message, too: "Cooking for others is a gracious thing to do—a giving of yourself. Cooking is sharing."

A sermon on the oft-told Christian story of the loaves and fishes a few years ago raised the question of whether Jesus' point was the miraculous creation of food (whether in a physical or a mystical sense) or the crowd's discovery "that when people share what they have, they will find there is enough to go around and then some." Many women recall their mothers following such an ethic, often extending hospitality, and sometimes to the poor. "My mom was the type of person that would feed the neighborhood if they were in need, or the roaming homeless," writes a thirty-eight-year-old who grew up in Texas. A fifty-year-old Iowan describes growing up in a poor inner-city area with "lots of kids. We had nine children but always had neighborhood children at mealtime." Her mother's message: "There's always enough to share." This woman's story reminded me of my own mother's willingness to include a friend of mine for dinner frequently during my early adolescence. My friend's parents worked virtually sixteen hours a day in their Atlanta business, leaving the four children to fend for themselves. A bowl of soup that the children heated from cans the parents bought by the case did little to satisfy my friend's need for a companionable evening meal. When this friend was at our house in the early evening, Mama always invited her to join us. Our full dinners, routinely prepared after Mama came home from work, were a welcome gift to her.

A retired Minnesota homemaker offers a memory of her mother's hospitality toward others throughout her life: "When I was going to school (especially high school), my friends were always welcome in our house to snack and for meals. There was always a large kettle of some kind of soup she had made, and on bread baking day we could snack (after school) on warm, just-baked bread and butter. When I was older (but before I married), on holidays, any friends of anyone in my family who had no place to spend the holiday were invited to spend it at our house." Jeanne E., interviewed with her mother, said she saw at the base of this message "kindness to other people . . . and doing for other people. [We learned that] if you had, you shared."

Jacqueline, a woman who, like me, grew up in Georgia, said in our interview, "I love [offering hospitality]; it's almost a gift that I'm giving." Asked about messages she got from her mother, she answered easily, "Everyone who came to our house was made to feel at home—welcomed by extending something to drink. Always." Jacqueline's sixteen-year-old daughter Jolawn, interviewed with her, echoed that strong message about hospitality when I asked what message her mother has passed down to her. Some anthropologists would add to Jacqueline's idea of offering food as a gift that it is indeed a gift, and more than a simple gift; it is a rather a " 'pure gift'—not trade, not barter, no strings attached."

My interview with Winn and her daughter Barbara S. focused a good deal on hospitality and its attendant virtues. Early in our conversation, Winn asserted her belief in the importance of food in offering hospitality: "I have a sense that sharing food is a spiritual experience. That's the reason I love to entertain people I want to nourish." Barbara echoed this commitment in discussing messages she received from Winn about the meaning of food in human relationships. "The most significant message is the importance of human connection and the idea of doing things for others, in this case of providing food or being in a role where you facilitate that, make that . . . happen."

Embedded in the theme of hospitality and sharing are those of generosity and inclusivity. These values came out in my discussion with Winn and Barbara about sharing not only food but also recipes. They related the experience of asking for recipes and being refused with the response "It's a family recipe, and I can't give that out." Such an exclusive attitude was so far removed from their own, inclusive, proclivities that it took them aback. Barbara remarked that "the notion that food is proprietary and that you don't share it, or the recipe for it, is totally alien." Later, she re-marked about having "a sense of family that's not enclosed."

Natalie related an incident in our interview that demonstrates how her mother Judy passed along the message of food's central place in offering hospitality. "When I first started working for the Jewish Federation in Chicago, my very first event was a full-day outing. It started with breakfast . . . , and then we were taking this steering committee of volunteers out to visit different agencies they funded. There was a horrible storm . . . , and the bus didn't show up, and we only got to see two of the three agencies. . . . I remember I called my mom that afternoon and I said, 'Oh, my God, you're not gonna *believe* this.' She said, 'What?' 'Well, all this stuff happened,' I said, 'blah, blah, blah.' She listened to me, and she said, 'Did the food arrive?' I said, 'Yes,' and she said, 'Then it was a success.' And I always use that when I teach my family education class. If there's food at a Jewish event, it's a success."

Some women of my mother's generation, born in the first quar-ter of the twentieth century, had mothers who were extraordinary role models for the message of offering hospitality. Lillian Smith writes in *Memory of a Large Christmas* of the year her mother agreed to have the chain gang to Christmas dinner, "Forty-eight men in stripes, with their guards." She and her sister helped her mother bake two caramel cakes and twelve sweet potato pies for the occasion. Likewise, Assata Shakur writes of the women of her grandmother's generation, "strong, fierce women," who "made giving an art form." Food examples predominate as Shakur shows how this played out: "Here, gal, take this pot of collards to Sister Sue." "Take this bag of pecans to school for the teacher." She goes on to say of these elders that "every child in the neighborhood ate in their kitchen." Shakur clearly views them with admiration.

Other writers of nonfiction reflect back on examples of hospi-tality on a smaller scale. Though she was raised by her grand-mother, when Maya Angelou was with her mother, she observed how much her mother valued both good food ("When they said cooking, they called Vivian Baxter's middle name") and offering food to guests. When a close friend called to say he'd be over, Maya's mother told her, "John Thomas is coming. . . . Please go get a couple of chickens from the kosher poultry store. Tell them to cut them up. . . . I'll whip up a few biscuits and give him some fried chicken," and she had her wooden bowl out, starting to make biscuits even before Maya was out the door.

Norma Jean and Carole Darden learned hospitality not only from their mother but from other women in their family as well. During summer visits as children, they helped their Aunt Norma clean house and set the table to prepare for "serving refreshments to the ladies from the Book and Garden Club" and other groups. Their mother, Mamie Jean Sampson Darden, "always cooked a little something extra in the pot for any unexpected guest."

As these examples demonstrate, the message to offer hospitality and share with others is inextricably bound up with food. Most women contributing to this book, from eighteen to eighty-eight, learned hospitality and value it. They may do the work of hospitality differently now than it was done in earlier times, sometimes having caterers provide the food, combining take-out with homemade food, or inviting guests to bring part of the food. It takes work, however it is accomplished. But offering hospitality has meaning for women that makes the work worthwhile.

## OFFER ABUNDANCE

The fourth most common message daughters report from their mothers is to provide plenty, or, in the words of a Maryland marketing professional, "Be generous; food should be abundant." A Michigan college student learned from her mother that it's "always better to make more than less." "You should try to serve way more than people will eat" was the message a Minnesota CPA received.

A sixty-year-old Louisiana woman's message emphasized the danger of cooking too little: "Cook enough; do not run out of food." The importance of planning enough food to serve becomes even a matter of ethnic pride, as illustrated by Beverly, who closed her interview by eyeing me severely and saying, "Just remember, Miriam. *God forbid* that a Norwegian woman should run out of food *at any time*."

One woman's commitment to offering abundance comes, if paradoxically, from her mother's practice of restricting the amount of food at the family table. Her mother's explicit message, in fact, was that overcooking is a sin! She had made of conserving food a vice. The daughter instead determined *not* to limit food offerings. She explained in our interview, "Maybe because of not having as much as I wanted, I want to have enough." She passed this transformed lesson, rather than her mother's explicit message, along to her own daughter, who echoed it in our conversation.

Offering plentiful food, a fundamentally positive tendency, can nevertheless take an unfortunate turn. While many women mention learning from their mothers the importance of gauging how much food is enough to serve others abundantly, some reflect that they—and others—were encouraged, even nagged, to eat more than they wanted. This problem was sometimes offered in response to the interview question "Are there connections around food with your mother that you have tried to avoid with your own daughter?" One woman replied thoughtfully, "I think there was always probably too *much* food." In a three-generation interview, the youngest mother present reported that her grandmother "threw the kids for a loop" by saying again and again, "Eat, eat, eat. There's plenty." "I knew about Grandma's way, but my children are not used to being pressed." Pressing too hard "blurs the line between encouragement and control," as another woman put it. Women who complete the survey question "The worst thing about my relationship with my mother around food is . . ." most often write such comments as "We eat too much" and "The tendency to overeat." Of the 67 percent writing a response to that question, 12 percent write of overeating when they get together with their mothers. Five percent write about their mothers pushing them to eat more than they want. A middle-aged woman laments one effect on herself of her mother's behavior: "I don't have to be hungry to eat!" Anthropologist Martin Loeb observes that giving a child food "seems to be almost as great a satisfaction as that of receiving it." Mothers take responsibility for—and pleasure in—feeding their daughters from birth, but some simply find it difficult to let go later in life.

Mothers can pass along their anxiety about food to their daughters, particularly questions of "How much is enough?" and "How much is too much?" Concerns arise about getting fat, on the one hand, and about starving oneself, on the other. Daughters writing such comments as "She is always looking at the calories and fat grams" and "She thought I was anorexic" indicate their mothers' focus on weight and diet. And sometimes mothers' ambivalence is apparent, as one woman remarks: "My mother sends mixed messages to eat a lot but not get fat." Such mixed messages reflect the inclination to feed, on the one hand, and social messages about body size and shape, on the other.

If, then, there are messages from *daughters* to *mothers* as they reflect on the messages they hear, they are "Don't push food" and "Don't worry about my diet!"

The four most commonly offered messages—to conserve, to make do, to share, and to offer abundance—all, interestingly, involve managing and using resources. The first pair focus on insuring that resources are used responsibly and creatively, the second on expansive use of resources. They balance one another nicely, and they apply to many areas of life outside the kitchen. Daughters who hear and appropriate messages such as these may acquire their implicit virtues as well—responsibility, self-reliance, generosity, and inventiveness.

## OTHER MESSAGES

While the four life messages above constitute nearly three-quarters of all messages in the survey pool, other messages appear commonly as well. *The importance of attractive presentation* came through to some women. Of her mother, a 28-year-old student/human service professional writes, "She always made us make up the table so it looked pretty. She always served food in serving dishes rather than pots or pans for . . . better presentation. . . . Dinner was a special time for us." From other mothers came the closely associated message that *family is special* and, therefore, family meals worthy of extra effort. A couple of middle-aged Pennsylvanians note this in their surveys. One learned that "Every meal is a special occasion, . . . that family is as special as guests, that food should be attractive, served in dishes, not wrappers, jars, cartons." The second writes of the foodstuffs that conveyed to her the message of family specialness: "My mother loved to bake and preserve—did grape juice, jams, jellies, made fudge. We had taffy pulls, and once a week she would make something special—beautiful pastries, iced cookies, gorgeous pies. These were not only wonderful to taste, but pretty to see." Some women specify the conditions appropriate for family meals—"no interruptions," "no phone use during meals," "no television (music is fine)." It is important, according to another, to nurture conversation because "good conversation goes with dinner."

Kevlyn, a thirty-eight-year-old homemaker, voiced a common message: *Be willing to try new things.* She recalled in a three-generation interview, "Mom really did try new things. She was really good about . . . trying foods. I remember when she got into her summertime cold soup phase. And that was great—gazpacho, vichyssoise. . . ." In another such interview, Lisa reminisced, "We had a variety of things. . . . Nobody else had fondue. That was really special. We had beef fondue, cheese fondue. Or we'd sit down and have a plate of artichokes. No one else [we knew] ever ate artichokes." Then, addressing her mother directly, she said, "I tell people that all the time, Mom, how lucky I was to have such a variety of food." In a third interview, Elizabeth R., another woman of Kevlyn and Lisa's generation, noted that her friends were "amazed" at the broad spectrum of foods she enjoyed at home, "Pomegranates—neat for kids." Other daughters spoke admiringly of how their mothers weren't "afraid to try something new or experiment," how "excitement would catch on when some really new . . . food would come to the table."

Older women remarked about their mothers' sophisticated taste as well. Jean mentioned avocados, and Elizabeth S. mentioned "ten-boy curry," a curry dish with ten individual condiments. Their reminiscences brought to mind the table of my childhood, where avocados and pomegranates were far from unusual. I remember vividly the basket of kumquats Mama brought home one Christmas during my preschool years—tart and sweet at the same time, and delicious.

Other messages worth noting concern *the value of method, persistence, and patience; the need to clean as one works; the desirability of using the best possible equipment and raw materials; and the importance of treating oneself.*

Most messages uncovered in the surveys and interviews may be characterized as positive, even wise, principles for living one's life. But not all. Seven percent of messages written by survey respondents are negative ones, or messages raising the problem of social roles relative to food. A few women, for example, report a message that can be summarized as "Men come first." A fifty-seven-year-old from Michigan writes, "My mother catered to my father's food whims. He was a picky eater. Meals were planned around his likes and dislikes [and around those of] my mother's brother when he came. I learned to cook for a man and to make my own likes and dislikes secondary. Men got bigger helpings and the best morsels. I got what was left—the less attractive and/ or burnt. I learned I was second class, not personally, but as a woman. Also, it was the woman's duty to plan meals, cook, and serve food to men."

A fifty-two-year-old Arkansas librarian remembers a similar message, "My brother and dad always got the chicken white meat, my mother ate the neck and the 'pope's nose.' ARGHH." "Men are to be served the best. Save the broken one for yourself. Always cook something Dad likes." These are the messages a thirty-nine-year-old educator remembers. Another, a sixty-year-old, notes that "Mother would *not* take the last chop from the serving plate for herself. I remember thinking how sad it was . . . and I didn't like it!" These women's experiences support DeVault's contention that gender roles dictate women's deference to men in food matters, irrespective of women's power in the kitchen. And messages to women to defer have permeated the culture. Reflecting the tradition of cooking what men like, for example, an old recipe book bears the title *To Make Him Say "Delicious!"*

No doubt related to lack of choice in the matter, or simply personal preference, some survey respondents' mothers disliked cooking and saw the necessity of performing that task, assigned automatically to them as "woman of the house," as a burden. They were "leashed down," in Sallie Tisdale's words.

- She was chained to cooking and she didn't like it much. My dad was unappreciative. (Minnesota writer-activist)

- My mother doesn't like to cook, prefers restaurants, and does not cook now unless it's a special occasion. [When I was] a kid, my mom would cook for us and serve us, then eat standing up in the kitchen! She definitely found the whole process a huge bore and resented having to do it. (Virginia administrative assistant)

- The worst thing is realizing, now that I'm grown, how much she disliked cooking. (Arkansas professional cook)

A message buttressing deference to men, then, is the idea that cooking is "women's duty," a theme mentioned by a few women.

In her study of Vivian Gornick's *Fierce Attachments*, Pearl David Laufer comments, "The kitchen is a woman's space when she chooses it for herself; it is her prison when her presence in it is obligatory and demanded by a man." But some women do not perceive a choice, given social messages, and some may not *have* a choice, given their circumstances. Most women surveyed—95 percent—do not subscribe to the statement "I believe it is a woman's place to cook for others." Nevertheless, in the majority of the households represented, women do most of the cooking. This finding is consistent with other research showing that women still bear most of the responsibility for cooking and household chores, men's increasing participation notwithstanding.

A forty-one-year-old who grew up in New York writes, "My mother resented cooking and I think it was a way she might have rebelled against the very traditional female role assigned to her." She continues, showing how social change and personal choice has resulted in a different experience for her: "As someone who has not followed a traditional path for women, I find I enjoy cooking quite a bit." Another daughter reflected that, while her mother's adherence to a strict routine of cooking the same dishes on a weekly schedule probably helped her survive a life of many demands, her mother "got stuck in ritualized food and relationships." When her parents were divorced, this daughter noticed, her mother broke out of that pattern. The lesson this daughter drew from her observation was "Please *yourself*."

These final examples show that, even as the positive predominate, some women receive messages that they consider negative from their mothers through food, often related to women's socially defined role. They resist the imposition of food-related "obligations and duties," and they do not want to take them on in the way their mothers did. Not surprisingly, then, in her study of young adult daughters and their mothers, Ann Caron found that, while those young women, products of a new culture, both like and try to understand their mothers, "they do not want to *be* their mothers."

Through social and economic change, many young women's lives both offer and require an array of roles, as well as resources to manage those roles. Freedom to choose figures prominently in their lives by comparison with their grandmothers' lives, and many reject intense involvement in traditional homemaking. Even women of their mothers' age exhibit this sentiment with specific regard to food:

- I've thought food was much too important to my mother. She was a good cook and seemed to think of it as the main female role in life. (Fifty-two-year-old college student)
- Food was too important. She was always thinking of the next meal. (Forty-eight-year-old college student)

Bobbie Ann Mason writes in her memoir that when she thinks of Clear Springs, Kentucky, her home town, she thinks first of "the women cooking." She remembers confronting her mother and grandmother about their constant focus on food.

One day Mama and Granny were shelling beans and talking about the proper method of drying apples. I was nearly eleven and still entirely absorbed with the March girls in Little Women. Drying apples was not in my dreams. [Grief] was weighing darkly on me at that moment, and I threw a little tantrum—what Mama called a hissy fit.
   "Can't y'all talk about anything but food?" I screamed.
   There was a shocked silence. "Well, what else is there?" Granny asked.

Mason goes on to say that while her grandmother didn't question "a woman's duties," she herself did. "I didn't want to be hulling beans in a hot kitchen when I was fifty years old."

As I write these words, newspapers around the country carry a news item released by the Future Homemakers of America (FHA) organization regarding a name change to Family, Career, and Community Leaders of America. Motivation for the name change came partly from a decline in membership (30,000 members in the five years prior to the press release) and partly from the "problem word" homemaker, which conjures up "images of stay-at-home housewives who cook pot roast and darn socks." Young women today want something different in life from what they perceive as "slaving over a hot stove." They may prepare food—survey results show they do—but few concentrate on food preparation the way even a working woman like my mother did in the forties and fifties. Signs of this change are all around us—in the transformation of grocery stores into semi-delicatessens, in the proliferation of take-out restaurants, in the rise of heat-and-eat entrees.

So times are changing. What children of the next generation—those born to the younger women of my survey sample—will learn from their mothers' messages is worth pondering. Since food is universal, it inevitably provides a place to learn not only practical skills, but also attitudes and values to take beyond the kitchen and the dining table to other arenas of life. As food mores change, what form and content will messages take? Clearly the women who contributed to this book received powerful, overwhelmingly positive messages about life—messages we need to hear—through food connections with their mothers. If food ceases to provide the medium it has in the past for this kind of learning, what will take its place?

Linda Gianoulis, a Minnesota woman, wrote to the *Star Tribune* when it asked for recipes for a special Mother's Day feature. She sent not a recipe but a story that is important to her: She cannot offer the taffy recipe that she would like to offer because her mother, Carol Olson, promised the woman who gave it to her sixty years ago that she would never give it out. (The recipe-giver's family was in the candy business.) Gianoulis wanted to tell the story "because it illustrates the person of commitment and integrity that my mother is. . . ." It is in ways such as Carol Olson's that mothers send life messages through food.

Daughters notice.

# 8

# *"Strength for the Journey": What We Take from Our Mothers*

In the introduction to her collection of letters between mothers and daughters, Karen Payne writes of what has been lost due to women's invisibility in history. "The saddest thing about it is how women have been deprived of a vital source of inspiration and self-esteem—that sense of pride which comes from appreciating the experiences and achievements of ordinary people like oneself." Historians and other students of women's lives are now working to uncover the lives of extraordinary "ordinary" women like many of those chronicled in this book. Those lives constitute a legacy for modern women.

In the preceding chapters, part of the legacy of women's work with food in particular is already laid out. The learning about food, the life lessons, the material objects—all are among the things women take from their motherline. But there is more. In this final chapter, I draw on a variety of sources, but especially on history and memoir, to look at women's achievements through food and how modern women make use of that legacy.

As Karen Payne points out, part of what women get from their mothers, and other women who came before, is inspiration, suggested by the admiration daughters express for their mother's accomplishments—including those surrounding food. Sometimes, admiration for apparently disparate activities is captured in a single statement. "We children loved her cooking as much as we loved her preaching," wrote Crystal Eastman, daughter of Annis Ford Eastman (1852–1910), the first woman to be ordained in the Congregational Church of New York State. Throughout history, the disparate activities have often dovetailed in food, whether prepared specifically for the family or on behalf of the family.

## THE LEGACY FROM THE HEARTH

It is easy for some daughters to identify with the child narrator in Martha Grimes' mystery *Hotel Paradise*. If not given to the hyperbole that their mother is "the best cook in the state," they nevertheless express their admiration in strong terms, writing that their mother is (or was) "an excellent cook," "a wonderful cook," "a great cook." Two Michigan college students write of their mothers, "Her cooking is the best I've ever tasted," and "She could make miracles in the kitchen." "No one could make food stretch so far and look so elegant," writes Marie Wilson, one of three authors of a study of transforming mothering. "She showed me you could create beauty and have fun with scarce resources." Other women offer more awe-full details:

- I will never be as good a cook as she was when she was my age. She always did her best to prepare good meals for me in my "growing up" years, even though she was working. I admire her greatly for that. (Fifty-six-year-old Georgian)
- My best recollection is of Fridays coming home from school. You could smell our place a block away due to all the baking my mom did. She also catered special events for friends. (New Mexico homemaker/marketing professional)
- I remember making cornbread as she called out the recipe to me [from another room as she did something else]. I could not believe that she could remember all that. (Texas contract administrator)
- I will always remember my mom in the kitchen with her apron on and wonderful smells filling the whole house. She'd always start two weeks before Thanksgiving and Christmas dinners to cook those meals, and every time was perfect. (Forty-four-year-old Louisianian)

In my interview with Kate L. and her mother, Mary M., the two remarked about the differences in their generations' approach to meal planning. Kate commented on the predictability of the dishes Mary served the family. "My sister and I were just naming off [our childhood food memories]: creamed tuna on toast, meatballs and gravy, pork chops, hamburger hotdish, meatloaf. . . ." These entrees would not work for Kate now, as a vegetarian. Far, though, from criticizing her mother for her predictable fare, she went on, looking at her mother as she spoke, "I was . . . marveling at you. You worked forty-plus hours a week and cooked! My sister's working, and she can't cook a meal. I'm not working full time, and I *barely* can. You [more or less cooked the same dishes for dinner every week] and didn't have to think. I think for every meal."

Kate's mother responded that her own childhood diet was even more structured than the one she offered her family: "We had [a standard dish for] each night of the week: Sunday, roast beef; Monday, hash; one night, hamburger hotdish, maybe pork chops. Friday, of course, we'd always have creamed tuna of one version or another, and on Saturday, we'd have hamburgers or hotdogs." Changing expectations about food—variety, quality, and preparation techniques—have made it more difficult for Kate and her sister to get a meal on the table. Still, Kate realizes what work it was for Mary to cook a family meal every night of the week, predictable though the fare was.

While Kate marveled at her mother's day-in and day-out provision of family meals, some daughters tell stories of occasions when their mother displayed a kind of "food heroism." Cokie Roberts has such a story about her mother. Lindy Boggs is an extraordinary woman, always active inside as well as outside the home, serving first on her husband's (Hale Boggs') Congressional staff, then as the first woman elected to Congress from Louisiana, and, more recently, as U.S. ambassador to the Vatican. Roberts writes that when she got married, her mother cooked *all the food for the 1500 people at the reception.*

Besides praise for their mothers' amazing feats with food—and their faithful production of quotidian meals—women tell stories of how mothers go the extra mile to make something special of the ordinary or to compensate for painful circumstances. Some mothers make the collective meal into an "event" by changing its setting. One fifty-one-year-old told a women's newspaper how her mother made picnics for the family to enjoy after the farm work was done. The menu, not unusual in its content, centered on meat-loaf, scalloped potatoes, and Jell-O. But this "twist" turned a reg-ular meal into an outing for a family with little money for extras.

The Darden sisters write of how their clever mother made trav-elling long distances by automobile as an African American family during the fifties not only tolerable, but fun. Mamie Darden made special shoebox lunches for the long journey south, knowing that, after a certain point (the end of the New Jersey turnpike), Blacks were not allowed in restaurants that served whites—virtually all of the restaurants on the road. She Scotch-taped the name of each family member to a shoebox to identify the box containing that person's lunch, including personal-favorite treats.

Sometimes, the painful circumstances mothers address with food are simply those of poverty. Gloria Wade-Gayles has "vivid memories of [Mama's] bargaining with the Italian market man over the prices of thin bunches of greens, too-hard okra, and po-tatoes that had too many eyes." Maymarie Calabrese told the (New York) *Daily News* that she is "still in awe" of her mother's ability to stretch what they had to feed a family of eight. She credits time spent in the kitchen with her mother with inspiring her own love of cooking. "She enjoyed making . . . nothing into something, because we were pretty poor back then." An Indiana clinical psychologist writes of what "a great role model" her mother was, "living in poverty but always eating lots of fruits and vegetables and being 5'1" tall and weighing 130 pounds even after having ten children."

Many women take pride in what their mothers did during the lean times of the first half of the twentieth century. One, a forty-year-old Massachusetts native, remembers her mother's view of her grandmother: "There are great associations with the Depres-sion, a large family, and food. . . . My mother lionized her mother's ability to make do, especially out of wartime rations, and to be generous (something my family found hard to do without complaint)." Some women, looking back on what their mothers had to contend with, feeding a family with little money, see the basic meals of their childhood home in a new light. One such woman, an Iowa county assessor writes, "We were poor. After I started home economics at school, I realized we didn't have a variety to choose from for meals. It makes me feel sorry for my mom. She had a very difficult task."

When writer Faith Sullivan was asked, in an interview about her work on the Depression era, whether women were as hard-working as she portrayed them, she replied this way:

My grandmother . . . was a working fool. She sold baked goods out of her house, besides keeping cows and chickens, which you were allowed to do in town in those days. All the women that I knew had golf-ball-sized knobs on their wrists during canning season: a cyst from using your wrist in a strenuous, muscle-working way. In the winter they would disappear, and the odd thing was nobody thought very much about them.

Thus is women's work in the family kitchen recalled by daughters who grew up in a variety of circumstances. Undaunted by barriers of poverty or race, of hard work and tedious routine, and even of vast numbers of people to be served, mothers such as the ones remembered here pressed on faithfully to sustain life and add to its pleasures.

## THE LEGACY FROM FARM WOMEN

Though the number of family farms shrinks daily, no account of women's work with food can ignore its place on the farm. Women's central position in the farm economy of days past is well documented by such historians as Mary Neth and John Mack Faragher. What is interesting about these historians' work is the extent to which it disproves a popular misconception of women's role in the farm economy. Faragher shows, in his work on the Midwestern farming family of the mid-nineteenth century, for example, how, "in fact, women were more centrally involved in providing subsistence for the farm family than men. Nearly all the kinds of food consumed by farm families were direct products of women's work in growing, collecting, butchering." And this was only a portion of the farmwoman's work, the "enormousness" of which Faragher emphasizes. He notes that though "a farmer was said to be a jack-of-all-trades, . . . women's work outdistanced men's in sheer variety of tasks."

*Frontier Woman: The Life of a Woman Homesteader on the Dakota Frontier* documents the personal saga of Grace Wayne Fairchild, a woman striving as "a homesteader in a dry country . . . raising a family without too much help of [her husband]." Describing how she had her "finger in a lot of pies" to produce income, Fairchild explains, "I had to make every penny I could or we wouldn't have made it." Historian Anne Webb shows, in fact, in her work on farming women on the Midwest frontier, that, some women were "doing it all." This was particularly true of homesteading (white) women, and women whose husbands abandoned the self-sufficient family farm ideal for material advancement through commercial farming, with all its risks. These women performed farm labor as well as domestic labor; moreover, they produced most of the family's food and brought in most of the cash earnings for living expenses through sale of products such as butter, milk, and eggs. Indeed, Webb writes, "As capitalism increasingly consumed white men's working lives, the virtues of independence and self-sufficiency were put into women's hands." She describes a different situation for American Indian women, since, by and large, Indian people did not adopt the commercial farming approach. Still, these women, too, grew and gathered food to barter with white settlers in order to sustain their lives and their families' lives.

Stephanie Coontz's account of the American family during the same period reveals how, as more and more work came to be removed from the home and men left farming or other family-owned businesses to move to centralized workplaces elsewhere, women were no longer involved in the same way in the home-based economy. In addition, they lost help with household work and childcare. Coontz shows how such women used their skills, including food-related skills, to contribute to family income. "Many women supplemented their household labor with income-generating work that could be done at or around the home—taking in boarders, doing extra sewing or laundering, keeping a few animals, or selling garden products."

Some farms did survive into the twentieth century, of course, and farmwomen continued to participate fully in that economy. Marjorie Myers Douglas, a woman who grew up in the city and never intended to leave it, found herself spending seventeen years on a farm unexpectedly when her husband's parents needed assistance to keep the family farm going. Her account of that experience allows the reader to see, through her eyes as a newcomer to farm life, what farmwomen's work involved.

Mother Douglas taught me to tend the garden, can produce, and make lavish meals for the farm crews in my big kitchen. She used to say, "A farm runs on food. Gasoline for the tractors, and food—lots of it—for the people. They work hard and deserve the best." I remember her quiet insistence on a large casserole of macaroni and cheese besides the tremendous amounts of pork roast and potatoes with glazed carrots, fresh peas, sliced tomatoes, and homemade bread and pie as noon dinner for the threshers.

Douglas continues, describing how she learned the wisdom of her mother-in-law, even as it contrasted with her own beliefs about food. She relates how, in a difficult year, Mother Douglas disguised hated mutton for a week's meals so that no one knew until she told them at the end of the week that it wasn't beef. She recalls her father-in-law's statement about farm life, "On the farm you'll never get rich, but you'll always eat well." And, as her book demonstrates, the women accomplished the task of bringing that food to the table with cleverness and creativity.

Bobbie Ann Mason details the meals her mother cooked for "the men" during harvest in Kentucky, halfway across the continent from the Douglas farm, and the part her mother played in producing what she cooked. The food, appropriate to the region, contrasts with that on the Douglas farm, but was an equally elaborate outlay.

Mama always preferred outdoor life, but she was a natural cook. At harvest time, after she'd come in from the garden and put out a wash, she would whip out a noontime dinner for the men in the field—my father and grandfather and maybe some neighbors and a couple of hired hands: fried chicken with milk gravy, ham, mashed potatoes, lima beans, field peas, corn, slaw, sliced tomatoes, fried apples, biscuits, and peach pie. This was not considered a banquet, only plain hearty food, fuel for work. All the ingredients except the flour, sugar, and salt came from our farm—the chickens, the hogs, the milk and butter, the Irish potatoes, the beans, peas, corn, cabbage, apples, peaches. Nothing was processed, except by Mama. She was always butchering and plucking and planting and hoeing and shredding and slicing and creaming (scraping cobs for the creamed corn) and pressure-cooking and canning and freezing and thawing and mixing and shaping and baking and frying.

Like Mason's mother, Beverly's North Dakota grandmother was much more interested in what was going on in the fields than in food for the table. Nevertheless, these meals needed to be tended to, so, during threshing, "she made sure the meals took place each day at 5 a.m., 10 a.m., 12 noon, 3 p.m., and 7 or 8 p.m."

## THE LEGACY FROM FOOD ENTERPRISE IN DAYS PAST

In historical accounts of both farm and non-farm women, the line between food for the family table and food as a way of providing family income blurs frequently. The kitchen served both as site for meal preparation and as workshop. And this happened throughout the country. Faith Sullivan's grandmother, mentioned earlier, lived in rural Minnesota; Lillian Smith writes of her childhood in rural Georgia that, when her family fell into poverty even before the Depression, her mother worked with her father to "make do," sending her Leghorns' eggs to town to be bartered for flour, cornmeal, and coffee. This work filled the larder with what the family did not produce for itself. As a result, "Mother could take cornmeal, mix it with flour, add soda and buttermilk and melted butter, a dab of sugar and salt, and present us with the best hot cakes in the world."

Winn recalled in our interview how her own mother really made survival possible for her Virginia family during the early part of the twentieth century. Winn's father, a travelling minister, refused raises, saying his wife "could manage." And manage she did. "Mother raised chickens in the backyard of a parsonage. We sold the eggs. . . . She was the glue that fed and kept the family. She even sold milk when we moved . . . to a farm. She had a cow that was very productive [and gave] rich milk. . . . Sometimes she made butter. She added to whatever Father was getting."

Neither Lillian Smith nor Winn was from an early-twentieth-century farm family proper. Women who were, though, show how enterprise with food continued, whether on a small or large scale. Bobbie Ann Mason helped pick the blackberries that her mother sold "to high-toned ladies in the big fine houses in [the nearby Kentucky] town . . . twenty-five cents for a quart of berries, a dollar a gallon." Marjorie Myers Douglas not only raised chickens for extra money on the family's Minnesota farm; chicken-raising ultimately became a serious sideline business. Her account of bungling the job of wringing a chicken's neck on first try brought back a vivid childhood memory. My cousin May killed a chicken this way quite effortlessly in front of my five-year-old eyes when my father took me to his family farm in 1946. As a child of the inner city, I was truly in awe (and still am) of that amazing feat—and of the many others women like May performed.

Women's contributions to family income, therefore, were not just for niceties; as Winn points out, they made the difference between survival and non-survival. An account of one woman's life in the mountains of Tennessee a century ago, a milieu in which tending the hearth was the only respectable option, suggests that women of her situation combined marriage with a career without even knowing it. "Vesta, A Modern Woman," as the recorder calls her, prepared "a table laden with food she had grown" in "a crude Tennessee valley." The list of enterprises she engaged in suggests the breadth of Vesta's work: "There were chicks to be hatched, a truck garden to be tended, eggs to be gathered, butter to be churned, cows to be milked—all of which meant food in the mouth and money in the pocket. Who could say she was not a breadwinner?"

Who indeed?

## MODERN USES OF WOMEN'S FOOD INHERITANCE

As contemporary women, we look back with amazement on women who wrung chickens' necks, butchered hogs, prepared six huge meals a day, and preserved a winter's worth of fruits, vegetables, and meats. Their lives seem far removed from ours. Multitudinous demands on women's time today make such focus on food impractical for most of us. How the connection between food and our motherline applies to modern life thus bears comment.

It is interesting, for example, how many women have taken inspiration from their mothers to pursue food-related enterprises and careers. Kava Zabawa and her mother began baking bread in 1969 to make some money when Zabawa's father died. They later opened a wholesale bakery operating out of a hundred-year-old farmhouse in the St. Croix River valley, on the Wisconsin-Minnesota border. Martha Stewart's mother taught her to cook and appears on her television show (sometimes correcting Stewart's kitchen techniques, I am told). Articles appear regularly in the popular press such as "Like Mother, Like Chef" (local chefs—some of them women—talk about their mothers' influence on their careers); "Bringing Home the Bakin' " (mother and daughter start biscotti business based on family recipes); "Fireworks and Family Fun" (East Coast restaurant owner and chef features Southern mom's recipes on menus); and "How I Did It" (how one woman turned a secret family recipe handed down since slavery into a multimillion-dollar business). Loretta Barrett Oden, co-owner of the Corn Dance Café in Santa Fe and member of the Pottawattaamie tribe, comments on how her heritage influenced her decision to become a chef:

What I really remember, most fondly, are the women in the kitchen. We would go out and gather what we called possum grapes and sand plums; the aunts would all get together and cook and see who could make the clearest jelly. They'd have competitions, and they'd enter their foods in the county and state fairs. It was just wonderful—the camaraderie, laughing, singing, and all of that in the kitchen! . . . These women were able to create, during times of plenty and times of famine, from the beginning of time. The women were the key to the survival of the people because they were the ones who were responsible for feeding and making food happen.

For these women, the influence of their mothers is quite apparent, and the daughters are fully aware of that influence. Most of us, though, do not pursue food-related careers. Nevertheless, we use what we observed and learned from our mothers in their work with food. As one woman put it, "She taught me life values, which I still share." The messages heard in mothers' approach to food, detailed in Chapter 7, help us along; ones such as "be ready," "plan ahead," "use the best materials," and "make do" apply in many endeavors. Maya Angelou recalls that in the early twentieth century, her grandmother "dared to divorce her husband and to support herself by carrying her five-cent meat pies across town in Stamps, Arkansas, to the men at the lumberyard and the cotton mill." Three years after she started, she bought land and set up a stand "midway between the two businesses and let the workers come to her." Angelou offers this story of this grandmother who raised her when she challenges women "to smile for themselves and to dare to venture into the unlikely."

I see in Angelou's grandmother self-reliance, toughness, and determination—qualities I saw in my own mother. Mama had the brains it took to develop a career as a dietician without benefit of a college education, and the strength and commitment it took to work in energy-sapping heat all day, then come home at night to make another hot meal for the family. And she kept her enthusiasm for food. One of the great regrets of her long-term illness later in life was that she couldn't work! From her example, I took patience, endurance, and a love of work—part of the underpinning, a launching pad in some ways, for my life.

What daughters absorb firsthand in the home kitchen is far from inconsequential. Besides learning foodways and life lessons, they may acquire a sense of language. This has served some women who write very well. "For the eventual making of literature," Grace Paley says, "my early life was probably healthy—lots of women in the kitchen talking, two strong languages, English and Russian in my ear at home, and the language of my grandmother and the grownups in the street—to remind me of the person I really was, the middle-class child of working people, the comfortable daughter of hounded wanderers, resting for a generation between languages." And, as Bettina Aptheker notes, Paule Marshall learned about "language as art" from her mother and her friends, domestic servants by day, homemakers by night. They met after work to talk.

The basement kitchen of the brownstone house where my family lived was the usual gathering place. Once inside the warm safety of its walls the women threw off the drab coats and hats, seated themselves at the large center table, drank their cups of tea or cocoa, and talked. While my sister and I sat at a smaller table over in a corner doing our homework, they talked—endlessly, passionately, poetically, and with impressive range. No subject was beyond them.

As Aptheker suggests, while kitchens see a lot of hard work, they are more than that. "[T]hey are also places of conversation, art, learning, light, warmth, and comfort," where a woman's standpoint emerges. Cokie Roberts believes her own daughter learned a great deal in the kitchen from her grandmothers. "Over sheets of cookie dough or stacks of campaign data, Becca absorbed the wisdom of older women and observed that intelligence does not depend on job descriptions." Rachel Naomi Remen's belief that wisdom—"the stuff that helps us to live a life worth remembering"—gets passed along at the kitchen table led her to name her best-selling book *Kitchen Table Wisdom*.

Some of what women take from times with Mother (and other family women) over food is intimacy with other women. "It is when we worked together in the kitchen that we were able to talk about things," writes a California secretary. "My mother and my sisters and I laughed and sang, and the boys and my father stayed away, making it an exclusive girl thing." A fifty-six-year-old Tennessee woman recalled similar occasions, "I loved going to my grandmother's house when all the aunts would get together and cook. What fun to share and laugh and work together!" A fifty-year old anthropologist's memory shows how just sharing food together facilitated intimacy. "My mother, sisters, aunts would frequently take food (such as ice cream) and all sit together or lie down together on my mother's king size bed and talk and laugh." Such scenes were recreated many times during my gathering of women's experiences.

Perhaps these scenes of intimacy and camaraderie account for a discovery I made looking at the surveys women completed. Reviewing what women regard as the best thing about their connection with their mothers through food, I was struck by the number of times the word, or word part, *joy* (as in *enjoy*) appears. Food is coupled with joy for many of us. Dorothy Allison ends her book of short stories *Trash* with a powerful afterword, portraying loving women cooking and eating together—and *enjoying* it:

I've been dreaming lately that I throw a dinner party, inviting all the women in my life. They come in with their own dishes. [Examples follow.] Everybody is feeding each other, exclaiming over recipes and gravies, introducing themselves and telling stories about great meals they've eaten. My mama is in the kitchen salting a vat of greens. Two of my aunts are arguing over whether to make little baking powder biscuits or big buttermilk hogsheads. Another steps around them to slide an iron skillet full of cornbread in the oven. . . . I walk back and forth from the porch to the kitchen, being hugged and kissed and stroked by everyone I pass. For the first time in my life I am not hungry, but everybody insists I have a little taste. I burp like a baby on her mama's shoulder. My stomach is full, relaxed, happy, and the taste of pan gravy is in my mouth. I can't stop grinning. The dream goes on and on, and through it all I hug myself and smile.

# CONCLUSION

In Chapter 1, I wrote of neglect in the literature of the positive link women have with their mothers through food and of apparent lack of interest in looking at the subject. Clearly, we have undervalued something precious. When I began to look into women's connections with their motherline through food, I had no idea how rich this legacy is. Reading hundreds of books and articles and, most important, listening to hundreds of individual women, then piecing together what the connections are, invoked in me profound respect for women who came before me. Though I relate most easily to Dorothy Allison's setting, above, I have been propelled into worlds I have little experience of—worlds like that of the Jewish women on the U.S. frontier, who kept a kosher kitchen against all odds, and that of mid-nineteenth-century farm women, who stirred constantly for hours, bending over a low open hearth, and who carried all the water for household use from well to house. I have seen the faces of women "pop" alert at the mention of women's connections through food—even women whose relationships with their mother is strained. And I know that this work has been worth the effort.

Alice Walker writes of her mother's activities, "She spent the summers canning vegetables and fruits." This she did, Walker adds, along with working in the fields all day and making all the clothes her children wore (even overalls) and all the bath and bed linen. Walker observes of her mother's life that "there was never a moment for her to sit down, undisturbed, to unravel her own private thoughts; never a time free from interruption. . . . And yet, it is to my mother—and all our mothers who were not famous— that I went in search of the secret of what has fed that muzzled and often mutilated, but vibrant, creative spirit that the black woman has inherited, and that pops out in wild and unlikely places to this day." She concludes, "We have constantly looked high, when we should have looked high—and low."

Like Alice Walker, many women contributing firsthand to this book, and other women whose voices are heard here from other sources, have found something more than nourishment for the body through the food link with their mothers and other women of their motherline. In the first mother-daughter interview I conducted, the pair discussed two ways of understanding food and what it means. Barbara S. addressed her mother: "There's a seriousness about food in your attitude. . . . It's not only spiritual; it's very practical. It's survival." Her mother responded by emphasizing the importance of food both in "enduring the living of every day" (the practical) and in "living gloriously" (the spiritual). She ended by saying, "It's the ideas that are nourished by eating together that provide you strength for the journey, that give you the relationships that provide encouragement, inspiration, challenge for living a bigger, better life."

As time goes by, I find myself thinking about my mother more and more. Her concern for nutritious food, well prepared, is in my thought. Her enthusiasm for food is in my heart, and her food wisdom is in my ears. I hear her Southern aphorisms on some subject nearly every day. I lived far away from her for most of our fifty years in common. But like Christina Garcia's fictional character Constancia, who left Cuba to live in the United States, I consider sometimes how far I traveled away from my mother, only to find she is waiting for me "in each new place." What she gave me through food, both for the body and for the soul, started me on my way and helps me get through every day.

During our interview with her three daughters, Ruth spoke with great energy of how passionately she feels about "the culture of food and what it does to create a civilized environment in which to raise children and in which people come together." She laments the neglect of the importance of food during the last half-century. So do I. For, indeed, that neglect has buried or ignored many women's contributions to creating civilized, and *civilizing*, life. It is time to uncover what we have buried or ignored, and to honor those women, excluded from public life and visibility, "to retain a living and true memory." To remember, though, we need to look, and we need to understand.

I have looked. And what I have understood is that, for all its

complexities, food's place in women's culture is a source of richness, a place where women's strength, intelligence, creativity, and
caring manifests itself day in and day out. I have understood the
depth of my own mother's gift to me through food, and that of
other mothers' gifts to their daughters. This is a tradition worth
learning from, commemorating, and celebrating. I have attempted
then, with the help of hundreds of women, to discover and show
some of the ways food connects mother and daughter, what it
means to us, and, in the process, to give women their due.

# *Reference Notes*

## CHAPTER 1

1    Title quote is from Virginia Woolf by way of Nice (1992, 183).

1    Anthropology provides interesting support for the "meals" with my late mother: Farb and Armelagos (1980, 76) suggest that "[n]o adults ever really eat alone, for always with them are the earliest eating experiences associated with the mother," and Bauwens (1978, 135) notes that, while occasional consumption of "soul food" (overlapping heavily the Southern food I name) affects health little, it offers satisfaction to the diner who grew up with it. Relative to the heavy overlap between soul and Southern food, the Minnesota friends I can talk with most easily about these meals are African American friends.

1    In "Connected to Mama's Spirit," Gloria Wade-Gayles recounts her aunt's words to her (1991, 237).

2    *Like Water for Chocolate* (1992).

2    Apter (1990, 1) writes about mothers' alleged crimes.

3    Exceptions to the neglect of broader mother-daughter connections through food include the work of British sociologists Blaxter and Paterson (1983).

3    In a review of the literature on affective characteristics of the mother-daughter relationship, Boyd (1989, 299) writes that "the data generally indicate that [it] is interdependent . . . , rewarding . . . , and close. . . ." My own research shows a positive feeling

among daughters for the relationship; nearly three-quarters of daughters surveyed find their relationship with their mothers satisfying.

3          Apter is the source of "the unwritten story" quote (1990, 34).

3          See Mellin, Irwin, and Scully (1992) and Story et al. (1991) for examples of documentation in the public health literature of the serious problem resulting when young women—even elementary schoolgirls—take drastic measures to attain socially elevated thinness.

3          Mintz (1996, 6).

3          *Like Mother, Like Daughter* is Waterhouse (1997), *My Mother Made Me Do It* is Fuchs (1989); women's personal accounts of eating disorders are included in such collections as Newman (1993).

4          Demos (1986, 31–35) provides an excellent summary of the ideal woman in the typical nineteenth-century American family.

4          Manton (1999, 5) asserts women's increasingly negative feelings about food. See Mintz and Kellogg (1988) for information cited on time spent in housekeeping and on social pressures on women related to proper homemaking. (See also Chapter 7 notes for related studies.)

4          Numbers of American women working outside the home are from estimates in Schor (1998, 115) using Bureau of Labor Statistics figures and *Current Population Survey* (March 1990). Note that estimates based on these records vary slightly in the literature.

4          Tilly and Scott are the historians quoted on women and family (1987, 2).

4          Vanek is quoted on allocation of household work (1980, 276).

4          Csikszentmihalyi reports adults' use of time, including amount of time spent on cooking proper and in household maintenance (1997, 44–45, 10–11).

5          DeVault found women retain responsibility even when men cook (1991, 139–42).

5          Scientist Ruth Hubbard's initial response to Avakian's appeal is given in Avakian (1997, 4–5). In later correspondence, Hubbard acknowledged that she came to understand why Avakian wanted to look at women's intimate connections through food but did not herself want to be involved since "food just has never been an avenue of [positive] communication for me" (6). Willoughby offers a snapshot of feminists' changing views on the value of studying cooking (1995).

5          Farb and Armelagos are quoted on the necessity of studying eating (1980, 4).

5          Mintz (1996, 3) comments on anthropologists' historic lack of interest in cooking and eating in Western societies. See Counihan

and Van Esterik for an overview of anthropological interest in food (1997, 1–2).

5     Mennell, Murcott and van Otterloo comment on sociologists' former neglect of the topic as insufficiently serious; they themselves find "food as a focus makes possible a very wide range of intellectual connections" (1992, 1, 118).

5     Burgoyne and Clarke comment on the absence of food in studies of family life (1983, 152). DeVault (1991) is a notable recent exception, examining in detail women's work feeding the family.

5     Forster and Ranum are the new historians of food quoted (1979, vii).

6     Comments about philosophy's neglect of the topic are from Curtin and Heldke (1992, xiv).

6     Beardsworth and Keil survey sociology's attention to food, including the recent surge of interest, due in part to "enhanced recognition by sociologists of the significance of domestic work and the domestic sphere in general" (1997, 4).

6     Mintz asserts the importance of food and eating (1996, 4).

6     Giard's words are from de Certeau, Giard, and Mayol (1998, 151).

7     Sources for the book's content range from informal talks with women, through searches of the literature of sociology, history, psychology, food science, public health, poetry, fiction, drama, autobiography, biography, folklore, cookery, and the popular media, to original research. Two focus groups, over simple meals, provided some of the first ideas, outside my own, for organizing themes. Next came interviews with a dozen pairs, or groups, of women in two- to three-generation configurations, involving a total of thirty-two women. Interviews followed a set of questions developed from themes emerging from focus group transcripts and related reading, with departures when other promising topics arose. Open-ended questions encouraged participants to pursue directions meaningful to them. I transcribed and studied the nearly 18 hours of interviews, which provided a check on themes from the focus groups and suggested others to explore.

A written survey widened the base of women directly involved. Friends, colleagues, and volunteers heretofore unknown to me distributed the survey around the country to book groups, church groups of women, college classes, corporate offices, and other groups, as well as to individuals. Responses from 412 women from all major U.S. census areas provide the database for survey results reported in the book. Women surveyed range in age from eighteen to eighty-eight, with an average age of thirty-nine. They reside in twenty-eight states and the District of Columbia, and in Canada. Their residence during childhood range across forty states, Canada, and four other nations. Nearly half have some college,

|      | but no degree. Six percent have a high school diploma or less, while seven percent have doctoral, law, or medical degrees. Thirteen percent are women of color. |
|------|---|
| 7    | I have tested some, but not all, recipes. |
| 8    | Nice's comment incorporates a phrase of Virginia Woolf's (1992, 183). |

# CHAPTER 2

| 9     | Quoted phrase in title is from Esquivel (1989, 15). |
|-------|---|
| 9     | Mintz writes of our absolute need for food (1996, 4). |
| 9–10  | *In Memory's Kitchen* is De Silva (1996). Quoted material is from De Silva's introduction (xxvi). |
| 10    | Esquivel (1989, 9). |
| 11    | Drewnowski, director of the human nutrition program at the University of Michigan, is quoted in Footnotes (1996). |
| 11    | Bauer quotes Kasper (1998, 14). Anthropologists agree with Kasper. Farb and Armelagos assert that "eating is closely linked to deep spiritual experiences" and offer examples (1980, 97). |
| 11    | Moore is quoted in Williams (1995, E1, 7). |
| 11    | *Babette's Feast* (1989) and *My Dinner with André* (1982). |
| 11    | Pert is quoted in Williams (1995, E1). |
| 11    | Hudnut-Beumler (1999) is the source of table grace quotation. |
| 11    | Mintz (1996, 8). |
| 11    | Daniel Sack reports on food in mainline Protestant churches in his work in Sack 1999 and Hudnut-Beumler (1999). His *Whitebread Protestants: Food and Religion in American Culture* came out late in 2000 from St. Martin's Press. For an interesting account of food in African American religious life, see Hughes (1997, 276–77). |
| 11    | Excerpt from the Christian scriptures is from Gold et al. (1995, 141). |
| 12    | Dean (1999b) is source of Marion Cunningham's words on dinner. |
| 12    | Berk and Berk offer information on primary family interaction time (1979, 219). |
| 12    | Doherty (1997, 27). Doherty treats in detail the place of rituals in building a family, including a chapter on family meals. |
| 13    | Miller, for example, suggests finding other interaction times when common meals are not possible (1990, 56). |
| 14    | Csikszentmihalyi reports feelings at mealtime (1997, 35). |
| 14    | Doherty is quoted on the "natural drift" of contemporary family life (1997, 8). |

14      Galinsky's *Ask the Children: What America's Children Really Think about Working Parents*, (1999a), is excerpted in Galinsky (1999b). Note that children want those routines and rituals; a Whirlpool Foundation (1998) study found that "having dinner together" and "going out to eat together" are two of children's favorite ways of being with their parents.

14      Beals studied children's vocabulary learning at the table (1997). A Harvard University Graduate School of Education study led by language development expert Catherine Snow found that young "children who participate in mealtime discussions later showed the highest aptitude for reading and vocabulary" (Marcus 1996).

14      Allen, Patterson, and Warren studied high school students (1970, 337).

14      Dreyer and Dreyer produced the figures on discipline at the family table (1973, 300).

15      Farb and Armelagos detail meal "rules" (1980, 110–11).

15      Gillman et al. (2000, 235) summarize the Harvard study's statistics on children's nutrition and family dining; the article's abstract has the clearest statistical results. Mintz (1996, 70) and Dreyer and Dreyer (1973, quote from 292) detail what they believe children learn at the table. The Dreyers' study is a particularly enlightening and detailed view of how dinner proceeds in middle-class North American families.

17      *Soul Food* (1997).

17      Stack (1974, 7–8).

17      Rossi (1995, 275).

17–18   Roberts (1999) is the source of the Kraft kitchen story.

18      Ackerman (1990, 127) is quoted on food's central place at significant events.

18      The long comment on holiday events in the family is from Shacochis (1994, 61). Writers like Colwin, on the other hand, write of conflicting feelings at holidays—"sibling rivalries, the unspoken resentments, the secret rages that occur even in the happiest families" (1993, 183–84).

19      For Smith's Christmas memories, see Smith (1962, 53, 74–76, 77, 78).

21–22   Melissa's comments are from Wilgocki (1996).

22      Roberts (1998, 188).

23–24   Holmgren (1998).

24–25   Broner (1993) describes the New York feminist Seder; quote is from the book's back cover.

25      Pomerantz (1998, 8, 10).

27          Danforth (2000, 1).

29          Williams is quoted in Iggers (1998, T2).

29          De Turenne summarizes statistics from the 1995 Roper poll and discusses changing dinner practices in the family (1996, T1).

29–30       Gillis (1996, 94).

30          The National Restaurant Association (N.R.A.) is an often-cited industry source of expenditures for meals bought away from home (1997a). N.R.A surveys suggest almost 40 percent of restaurant *users* say "meals prepared at a restaurant are essential to the way they live." (Italics added; I have seen N.R.A. statistics on restaurant *users* reported as representing the general population.) Further, their survey of those customers showed that nearly one-half are cooking fewer meals than they were two years ago. Note that the percentage of restaurant users saying restaurant meals are essential . . . rises from 38 percent among eighteen- to thirty-four-year-olds to a high of 60 percent among fifty-five- to sixty-four-year-olds. From age sixty-five, the percentage begins to decline to 54 percent (1997c). N.R.A.'s analysis of Department of Labor data shows our per capita expenditure for food away from home in 1995 (the most recent available figures) was $681 (1997a). But "frequent dinner customers," including those buying fast food and carryout food, account for 74 percent of all dinners eaten out (1997c). N.R.A.'s figures on non-frequent dinner customers, on the other hand, are close to women responding to my survey; they average 1.3 dinners out a week (1997b).

30          Newport (1997) reports the 1997 Gallup poll replicating one of fifty years earlier. Gillman et al. (2000, 235) report results of the Harvard Medical Schoool study on children's dinners with the family (see abstract for best summary of statistics).

30          Source of information on the survey of U.S. workers is Bond, Galinsky, and Swanberg (1998, 6).

30          Galinsky reports what children think and shows how their accounts of family meals taken together differ from their parents' (1999a, 84, 73–77).

30          Bauer (1998) is the source of Kasper's words on the table.

31          Glickman (1993).

32          Teacher-chef Jonathan Zearfoss is quoted in Williams (1995, E7).

33          Paul (1998).

33          Hochschild with Machung (1998, 784).

34          A forty-one-year-old Michigan woman is the source of the quotation in the chapter's final paragraph.

# CHAPTER 3

35          The title quote is from the open-ended survey question, "The best thing about my relationship with my mother through food is . . . ," to which more women write a communication-based answer than any other.

37          Manton (1999, 58) calls the kitchen the emotional center of the home.

37          Giard's discussion of kitchen time is in de Certeau, Giard, and Mayol (1998, 191).

38          Steph's story is from Wilgocki (1996).

39          Bateson (1989, 134, 126, respectively).

40–41       Wade-Gayles' kitchen story is from Wade-Gayles (1991, quotations 291).

41          Apter (1990, 67).

41          Douglas (1994, 125–26).

41–42       Hughes (1997, 273).

42          Grimes (1996, 138–39).

42–43       Colette (1966, 22).

45          The "Sally Forth" cartoon described was published July 11, 1999, ©1999, King Features Syndicates, Inc.

47          Farb and Armelagos (1980, 4).

47          Roberts (1998, 164) gives no source for the survey in her book.

47–48       Ng (1998, 239–241, 252).

48          Selingo (1999) reports historian Yong Chen's work.

50          Fischer (1986, 95).

51          Letters between mother and daughter may not be as appropriate as is commonly believed. Contrary to the popular belief that families are separated more and more due to mobility of the population, Uhlenberg (1995, 22) shows how information from the U.S. Bureau of the Census and other surveys document that mobility rates have lowered since the 1960s and that "about 75% of parents older than 65 have a child living within a 25-mile radius of them."

52          Caron (1998, 88).

52          Sherline (1993, xii–iii).

52–53       Payne (1983).

53          Isa Kogon's letter is in Payne (1983, 266–69, quoted words 268–69).

53          Bernard's letter is in Payne (1983, 269–71), originally published in J. Bernard, 1978, *Self-Portrait of a Family*, Boston, Beacon Press.

# CHAPTER 4

55          The title quote is Joyce Maynard's (1995).

55          Boswell's comments on human nature are originally from *Journal of a Tour to the Hebrides with Samuel Johnson, L.L.D.*, ed. R.W. Chapman, London, Oxford University Press (1930, 179), cited in Farb and Armelagos (1980, 228).

55          Allport (2000, 122, 123).

55          A review of research demonstrating the assignment of food duties to women may be found in Mennell, Murcott, and van Otterloo (1992).

55          While 61 percent of all women surveyed prepare meals everyday, 78 percent of women living in a household with men do so.

56          Neisser reports that mothers of the Hopi of Northern Arizona and Kenya's Gusii train their children directly (1969, 286–91, 314–17).

56          Spruill reports on eighteenth-century women's training (1982).

56          Smith-Rosenberg reports on Victorian mother-to-daughter training (1985, 33, 65).

56          For a variety of reasons, including absence of a compelling need, women do not acquire food skills to the extent that all children acquire their native language.

57          Giard's words are in de Certeau, Giard, and Mayol (1998, 191).

57          Peggy's comments are from Wilgocki (1996).

58          Ehrlich (1997, xii, 265).

59          Stillman's story is related in Phill (1999a).

59          Bauwens (1978, 134).

59          Bateson (1989, 133).

60          It is not surprising that women are not taught how to coordinate menu items for a meal, since, as Berk and Berk (1979, 9) note, we know almost nothing about how this is done.

62–63       Carothers is the source of the three quotations (1998, 320).

63          Allison and Duncan are the source of statement on flow in motherhood (1988, 129).

63          Brenda Langton is quoted in Holiday memories (1996, 27).

63          The "Sally Forth" cartoon described is ©1996 Greg Howard, published December 25, 1996, distributed by King Features Syndicate.

64          Christensen's story is told by Thorson (1996b).

64          Beach's story is told by Phill (1996a, T1).

64          Lalli's story is in Robison (1997, 115).

65          Smith (1962, 73–74).

65            Regarding observed correlations, precise results from tests of sta-
              tistical significance are not reported here or elsewhere because the
              survey results were not obtained through random sampling, and
              are not therefore generalizable to the entire population of adult
              women in the U.S. Having acknowledged that, however, I have
              observed very similar results for both my survey and scientific
              polls such as ones done by the Gallup and the Roper organizations
              on certain issues, such as those associated with family dining prac-
              tices. These similarities give me confidence in my results.

65            M.F.K. Fisher's story is excerpted in Chernin (1985, quotes from
              111).

66            Darden and Darden (1978, 61).

67            Reichl's childhood in food is described in Sutel (99, E1). *Tender at
              the Bone* is Reichl (1998, quote on 5). Employing a cook was more
              common, even in middle class homes, when social and economic
              conditions required the poor, especially women of color, to take
              jobs as domestics.

68            Arcana interviewed 120 women for her study of mothers and
              daughters and included comments from daughters about their
              mothers' competitiveness with regard to food (1979, 98, 104).

68            Counihan and Van Esterik are the anthropologists quoted on con-
              trol of food (1997, 3, 110).

68            Csikszentmihalyi (1997) describes cooking as a relatively positive
              experience (38).

68            Manton, for example, notes the lack of "a room of one's own" for
              women (1999, 58).

68            Csikszentmihalyi (1997) correlates kitchen time with best moods (44);
              most negative experiences are described (58). There may be class dif-
              ferences, however, in how even cleaning chores are experienced.
              Allison and Duncan found that blue-collar women enjoy the control,
              routine, and "rootedness" of home, by contrast with middle-class
              women who work outside the home and may experience more con-
              trol in the workplace. One blue-collar woman is quoted as saying,
              "When dinner is ready on time, and the house is clean—the routine
              is nice to have in family life, to have play time in the tub, play time at
              the table—it gives you a rootedness, a routine" (1988, 131).

69            Mason (1999, 83, 112).

70–71         Hochschild with Machung (1998, 784) reports Pesquera's work,
              *Work and Family: A Comparative Analysis of Professional, Clerical and
              Blue Collar Chicana Workers*, Ph.D. diss., University of California,
              Berkeley, 1986.

72            Smith's *The Journey* is excerpted in Olsen (1984, 175).

72–73         See Manton for a discussion of home economics classes as a tool
              for food reformers attempting to change the American diet away

from traditional food and toward one more in line with domestic
science (1999, 48–50).

73  Catherine's *American Home* ... cookbook is Habeeb and staff
(1966).

74  Marje Jaasma, Personal communication (March 12, 1998).

74  Lydia Bothan, director of consumer affairs and test kitchens at
Land O'Lakes, is the food industry expert quoted in Neidorf (1996,
6).

74  *Joy of Cooking* is Rombauer, Becker, and Becker (1997).

74  Colwin (1993, 126).

74  Dean is source of Foster story (1998a, T6).

74  Ironically, in spite of Marion Rombauer Becker's gracious tributes
to her mother in later editions of the book, these two had a less
than joyful relationship, according to A. Mendleson's account in
*Stand Facing the Stove*, reported in Durbin (1997).

75  Colwin (1993, 126).

75  Anderson (1982, 93) comments on daughters' influence on mothers.

75  Phill (1997a) is the source of a mother's comments on how her
daughter taught her to change.

78  Caron (1998, 89) quotes the mother on deferring to her chef daughter.

79  The "Stone Soup" cartoons, (c) Jan Eliot, were published in early
October 1998, distributed by Universal Press Syndicate; the cartoon quoted was published October 8.

79  Eckstein (1980, 500–501).

# CHAPTER 5

81  Title quote is suggested by Mira's mother's letters (Payne 1983,
343–51).

81–82  Shacochis (1994, 187–88).

82  Roberts (1998, 104).

82  Spruill (1982, 33).

82  A precise total of named sick foods and drinks is unavailable,
since I coded only the first four items named by any respondent
for the descriptive statistics, and some respondents named more
than four.

82  Burros (1999) reports on scientific studies of chicken soup's benefits. Parents interested in what experts recommend for sick children may examine such sources as Roberts, Heyman, and Tracy
(1999).

| | |
|---|---|
| 83 | Roberts (1998, 157). |
| 84 | Colwin (1988, 106–10). |
| 84 | Breathnach (1995, July 7 entry, unpaged). |
| 84 | "Home cooking" cookbooks named are Brown (1996) and Burkhard (1998). |
| 85 | The difference between the rankings of baked sweets and meat is small—1.5 percentage points. |
| 85 | Eversole's story is told in Franklin (1996). |
| 90 | As with sick foods and drinks, a precise total of named comfort foods and drinks is unavailable, since I coded only up to five items named by any respondent. The total number is in the range of 950 to 1000. |
| 90 | Farb and Armelagos are the anthropologists quoted (1980, 73). |
| 91 | Hergstriet's letter is in Payne (1983, 287–89, quote on 288). |
| 91 | Dean (1998b) is source of quote on universal expression of love. |
| 91 | Breathnach (1995, July 8, unpaged). |
| 92 | Custard story is from Sicherman (1999, T6). |
| 92 | Cannon's comments are from Lawrence-Lightfoot (1994, 82). |
| 92 | Lightfoot (1988, 18). (Lawrence-Lightfoot hyphenated her name between her 1988 and 1994 books.) |
| 92 | Douglas (1994, 125). |
| 92–93 | Angelou (1975, 63). |
| 93 | Payne (1983, 143) is the source of Eastman family letters, reprinted from a private collection, ©Yvette Eastman. |
| 94 | Letters between Mira and her mother are in Payne (1983, 343–51). |
| 95 | Hebrew prayer is from Cardin (1988). |
| 95–96 | Darden and Darden (1978, 187). |
| 97 | Fisher's words from the foreword to *The Gastronomical Me* are quoted in Shacochis (1994, 7). |
| 97 | Daniel and Effinger quote the source on bosom biscuits (1996, 192). |
| 97–99 | Hull is the source of "The Taste of Mother Love" and "8-5-88" (1989, 2–3, 140, respectively). |
| 99 | Yezierska (1975, 165–66, 170–71, 172). |
| 99 | Lawrence-Lightfoot (1994, 3). |
| 100 | Sklar's story is "Passing Away" (1996, quote on 115). |
| 100 | Franzmeier is quoted in Wilbur (1998, 12). |
| 100 | Cooper (1998, 143, 144) quotes executive chefs Lidia Bastianich and Susan Regis. |
| 100 | The mad food proverb is in Phill (1996b). |

100            Khan (1991, 190) is source of quote on Hindu thought.

100            Comments on cook's state of mind are from Khan (1991, 189).

100–101     Chisti (1991, 43) discusses Sufi healers' concerns.

101            Cunningham's misgivings are in Dean (1999b).

101            Walker studied women's lives through their letters and comments
               on social expectations for women (1996, 37). DeVault (1991) shows
               how expectations regarding feeding others serve to maintain un-
               equal relations between women and men.

101            Gillis (1996, 178).

101            Prior-Nolan (2000) is the source on Minneapolis's Wedge Coop.

102            Cowan (1982, 332).

102            Bateson (1989, 128, 123, 136). Manton believes women might well
               "take a more active hand in the preparation of the food they both
               eat themselves and offer to those they love" as a means of "nur-
               turing self and others" to regain control over their nutrition (1999,
               112–13).

103            Allport (2000, 200).

103            Yoshimoto (1988, 75).


# CHAPTER 6

105            Title quote is from Remen (1996, 266); she recounts the story of
               one woman's sense, as she prepared her first Passover as an adult,
               of being in a stream of five thousand years of Jewish women.

105            *In Memory's Kitchen* is De Silva (1996; quote from Anny Stern is
               on xxvii).

105            Lowinsky (1992, 4, 99).

106            Maynard (1995).

106            Leeson (1999).

106            Willits (1996, T2).

106–7        Grosvenor's words are in Smart-Grosvenor (1992, 295).

107            Walker (1997, 220, 219, 217).

108            Meier (1997) reports on *Who Gets. . . .*

108            *In Memory's Kitchen* is De Silva (1996).

110            Sicherman's *Star Tribune* article contains Mother's Day recipes and
               stories (1999, T1, 6–7, quote T1).

113            Carol Leach's story is from Phill (1999b).

114            North (1993).

114            Judy Goldfein's words are in Goldfein (1994, 1, 4).

116            *At Martha's Table* (1997).

| 116 | Darden and Darden (1978, ix, xi). |
| 116–17 | Hughes (1997, 273). |
| 117 | Egerton (1987, 37). |
| 117 | Manton (1999, 112, 89). |
| 117 | Hughes (1997, 273). |
| 117 | Heldke (1992, 257). |
| 118 | Lightfoot (1988, 20, 10). |
| 119 | When my local paper asked, in 1997, for stories about mothers and food for a Mother's Day food feature, oddly, they received few responses (Lee Svitak Dean, *Star Tribune* food editor, personal e-mail communication, July 11, 1997). In 1999, however, when they asked for recipes for a similar feature, they found they received *lots* of recipes—*with stories* (Sicherman 1999). The different results may have been due to the form the newspaper's requests took. If people start by simply copying a recipe, this act may bring to mind certain memories, which they then proceed to relate. In any case, the light response to the call for memories probably has less to do with a lack of memories than with not having time, and perhaps not preferring, to write. My experience in obtaining oral and written contributions to this book was that many fewer women, proportionately, wrote answers to the reflective questions in the written survey than offered them orally in other research settings. |
| 119 | Allison (1988, 152). |
| 120 | Farb and Armelagos (1980, 110) discuss for example how for the Romans white bread "symbolized well-being and prosperity." |
| 120 | Hale's story is in Phill (1997b). |
| 121 | "Rosey's" is from White (1993, 3–5). |
| 121 | "Dead on the Road" is from White (1993, 39–40). |
| 123 | Buchholz (1997) is source of food-as-heirloom quotation. |
| 123 | Roberts (1998, 7). |
| 123 | Giard's words are from de Certeau, Giard, and Mayol (1998, 153). |
| 124 | Ehrlich's *Miriam's Kitchen* is the memoir quoted (1997, 150). |

# CHAPTER 7

| 125 | Title quote is from Barbara S., interviewed with her mother. |
| 125 | Walker (1998). |
| 126 | Messages quoted from the survey include answers both to a question specifically aimed at messages and to other open questions (e.g., "The best thing about my relationship with my mother is/was . . ."). |

129            Smith (1962, 77).

131            Bateson (1989, 3–4).

131–32         Giard's words are from de Certeau, Giard, and Mayol (1998, 151).

132            In her study of feeding affluent and poor families, DeVault (1998, 185–86) points out how differently women experience making do, depending on the means available to them.

132            Hughes (1997, 276).

132            Cooper (1998, 34) quotes Lewis. John Egerton adds a note on Black creativity with food, based in social history. He writes that the Southern kitchen was one of the few places that Blacks (and white women) were able to "let their guard down and be themselves. Almost everywhere else, they had to conform to binding roles that stifled their expression and killed creativity, but in the kitchen, they could be extravagant, artistic, whimsical, assertive, even sensuous" (1987, 17).

132            Yezierska (1975, 251).

133            Jerry Lane's unpublished homily at the Church of St. Stephen, Minneapolis, is quoted (August 3, 1996).

135            Relative to Judy's remark about the central place of food at Jewish events, Cantor (1995, 67) discusses the importance of food in Jewish life, because of concern for "preserving individual life and the commitment to group survival.... Through feeding, Jews symbolically gave themselves and each other the love, nurturing, and caring they needed to offset/counteract outside hostility."

135            Smith (1962, 60).

135            Shakur and Chesimard (1978, 13–14).

135–36         Angelou (1975, 104).

136            Darden and Darden (1978, 81–82, 185).

136            An interesting connection to women's concern with not running out of food is Allport's observation that only the female of a number of species, including chimps, hoards food (2000, 69).

136–37         See Anderson (1982) for a broader use of the question about avoiding with one's daughter(s) behaviors observed in one's mother.

137            Loeb comments on the pleasure of feeding a child (1951, 227).

140            DeVault (1991); note also that British sociologist Anne Murcott (1983) found that British young women defer to their husbands' preferences (182) and that "cooking is securely anchored as the responsibility of women as wives and as mothers" in the households she studied (181). Farb and Armelagos show how, universally, "eating is intimately connected with sex roles, including who gets served first" (usually males) (1980, 5). The cookbook described is on display in Grand Manan Island's (Newfoundland)

historic museum, undated, published by Gunns Limited in Toronto, a producer of vegetable shortening.

140     Tisdale (2000, 99).

141     Laufer (1989, 124).

141     My own data about which sex does the cooking in households are
        somewhat confounding; more people do not check "Cooking in
        my household is done mostly by females" than can be accounted
        for by answers to related questions—"Cooking in my household
        is done mostly by males," "Members of my household share cook-
        ing duties equally," and "Not applicable" (for one-person or one-
        adult households, for example). The complete picture is therefore
        shadowy. Related studies of household labor are reported in Va-
        nek (1980); Berk (1980) includes a number of articles relevant to
        the topic, especially Robinson's work showing the relative amount
        of time women and men spend in household work, including
        food-related activities; Glazer (1980) explores some of the reasons
        why women spend more time in household work, including cook-
        ing; Berk and Berk (1979) show how women's and men's employ-
        ment affects their use of time; and Csikszentmihalyi's time studies
        offer relevant data (1997, 10–11 and 44–45, especially).

141     Beardsworth and Keil (1997, 86) summarize some feminist soci-
        ologists' view of food-related roles. They identify two basic
        themes—that food roles both express and reflect women's sub-
        ordination and that the resulting obligations and duties serve to
        enforce that subordination.

141     Caron (1998, 4).

142     Mason (1999, 82).

142     Future homemakers (1999).

143     Barbara Haber, curator of books at Radcliffe's Schlesinger Library
        on the History of Women, notes that food has served as an im-
        portant ground for passing along values in the family (Willoughby
        1995).

143     Sicherman (1999, T6) tells Gianoulis' story about her mother.

# CHAPTER 8

145     The title quote is from Winn, interviewed with her daughter.

145     Payne (1983, xv–vi; quote from Eastman letter is from 141).

146     Grimes (1996, 5).

146     Marie Wilson's words are quoted from Debold, Wilson, and Ma-
        lave (1993, xii.)

147     Roberts (1998, 160).

147–48  Wilgocki (1996) tells the farm family's picnic story.

148            Darden and Darden (1978, 246). The Dardens' chapter "On the Road" honors friends—old and newfound—who fed them on their journeys. Anthropologist Martin Loeb pointed out in his mid-twentieth-century study of the social functions of food habits that "[t]here is probably more discrimination in eating places and around eating habits than anything else in America" (1951, 229).

148            Wade-Gayles (1991, 222).

148            Calabrese's testimony is in Han (1998).

149            Sullivan's interview is in Carter (1996).

149            Neth (1995) and Faragher (1982) are examples of work documenting women's position in the farm economy.

149            Faragher (1982, 118, 123, 120).

149–50         Wyman uses Grace Fairchild's notes and letters to tell her story (1972, quotes 109).

150            Webb (1997), Chapter 5, "Farm Wives," "Farm Wives and the Yeoman Ideal" section, unpaged.

150            Coontz (1997, 55).

150–51         Douglas (1994, 36–37).

151            Mason (1999, 84).

151            Webb (1997, unpaged) describes women's contributions through meals to the farm economy and the symbolic value of enormous feasts.

152            Smith (1962, 58–59).

152            Mason (1999, 4).

152–53         Douglas (1994, 167–73).

153            Vesta is remembered in Winter (1965, 31–32, quote on 31).

154            Stories of women's entrepreneurial ventures with food are, in order of appearance in text, Perkins (1996); Martha Stewart is closing . . . (1996); Thorson (1996a); Bendrick (1996); Ellis (1996); and How I did it (1998).

154            Ann Cooper's study of women chefs is the source of Loretta Barrett Oden's words (1998, 54).

154–55         Maya Angelou's story about her grandmother is in DePass (1998).

155            Paley's words are recorded in Taylor (1990, 3).

155            Marshall's words, from a 1983 *New York Times Book Review* article, are quoted in Aptheker (1989, 49–50).

156            Roberts (1998, 163).

156            Remen (1996, xxvii).

156–57         Allison (1988, 164–65).

| | |
|---|---|
| 157 | Schloff (1996) offers an engaging account of Jewish women's work and life on the frontier. |
| 157 | Faragher describes the backbreaking world of antebellum Midwestern farmwomen (1982, 119). |
| 157–58 | Walker (1983, 238–39). |
| 158 | Garcia (1997, 132–33). |
| 158 | Giard's writes of the need for a living and true memory of women in de Certeau, Giard, and Mayol (1998, 153). |

# References

Ackerman, D. 1990. *A natural history of the senses*. New York: Random House.

Allen, D.E., Z.J. Patterson, and G.L. Warren. 1970. Nutrition, family commensality, and academic performance among high school youth. *Journal of Home Economics* 62:333–37.

Allison, D. 1988. *Trash*. Ithaca, N.Y.: Firebrand Books.

Allison, M.T., and M.C. Duncan. 1988. Women, work, and flow. In *Optimal experience: Psychological studies of flow in consciousness*, ed. M. Csikszentmihalyi and I.S. Csikszentmihalyi, 118–37. New York: Cambridge University Press.

Allport, S. 2000. *The primal feast: Food, sex, foraging, and love*. New York: Harmony Books.

Anderson, R.M. 1982. Mothers and daughters: Their adult relationships. Ph.D. diss., University of Minnesota.

Angelou, M. 1975. *Gather together in my name*. New York: Bantam Books.

Apter, T. 1990. *Altered loves: Mothers and daughters during adolescence*. New York: St. Martin's Press.

Aptheker, B. 1989. *Tapestries of life: Women's work, women's consciousness, and the meaning of daily experience*. Amherst: The University of Massachusetts Press.

Arcana, J. 1979. *Our mothers' daughters*. Berkeley: Shameless Hussy Press.

*At Martha's table*. 1997. Privately printed by the Stadther family.

Avakian, A.V., ed. 1997. *Through the kitchen window: Women explore the intimate meanings of food and cooking*. Boston: Beacon Press.

*Babette's feast*. 1989. Produced by J. Betzer and directed by G. Axel. Orange City, Calif.: A.S. Panorama.

Bateson, M.C. 1989. *Composing a life*. New York: Penguin Books.

Bauer, A.M. 1998. Lynne Rossetto Kasper: An appetite for life. *Minnesota Women's Press*, 10 November, 14–15.

Bauwens, E.E. 1978. *The anthropology of health*. St. Louis: The C.V. Mosby Company.

Beals, D.E. 1997. Sources of support for learning words in conversation: Evidence from mealtimes. *Journal of Child Language* 24:673–94.

Beardsworth, A., and T. Keil. 1997. *Sociology on the menu: An invitation to the study of food and society*. New York: Routledge.

Bendrick, M.L. 1996. Bringing home the bakin'. *Active Times*, Summer, 5–6.

Berk, R.A., and S.F. Berk. 1979. *Labor and leisure at home: Content and organization of the household day*. Beverly Hills: Sage Publications.

Berk, S.F., ed. 1980. *Women and household labor*. Beverly Hills: Sage Publications.

Blaxter, M., and E. Paterson. 1983. The goodness is out of it: The meaning of food to two generations. In *The sociology of food and eating: Essays on the social significance of food*, ed. A. Murcott, 95–105. Aldershot, Hants, England: Gower.

Bond, J.T., E. Galinsky, and J.E. Swanberg. 1998. The 1997 national study of the changing workforce: Executive summary. New York: Families and Work Institute. Available from http://*www.familiesandwork.org*.

Boyd, C. 1989. Mothers and daughters: A discussion of theory and research. *Journal of Marriage and the Family* 51:291–301.

Breathnach, S.B. 1995. *Simple abundance*. New York: Warner Books.

Broner, E.M. 1993. *The telling*. San Francisco: HarperSanFrancisco.

Brown, T.D. 1996. *The homespun cookbook: Comfort food favorites from the heart of America*. New York: Berkley Publishing Group.

Buchholz, B.B. 1997. Food, recipes and rituals: The bond of past and future generations of cooks. *Chicago Tribune Magazine*, 9 November, 16.

Burgoyne, J., and D. Clarke. 1983. You are what you eat: Food and family reconstitution. In *The sociology of food and eating: Essays on the social significance of food*, ed. A. Murcott, 152–63. Aldershot, Hants, England: Gower.

Burkhard, J. 1998. *The comfort food cookbook*. Buffalo, N.Y.: Robert Rose Inc.

Burkman, M.A., M. Balakshin, and R. Klugman. 1995. "Now we're cooking!" program: Helping schools, communities, and families make meals matter. *Journal of Nutrition Education* 17:216B-C.

Burros, M. 1999. Will chicken soup bowl over the flu? *Star Tribune*, 10 February, Taste section, T3.

Cantor, A. 1995. *Jewish women/Jewish men: The legacy of patriarchy in Jewish life*. San Francisco: HarperSanFrancisco.

Cardin, N.B. 1988. A Woman's prayer from the 18th century. *Lilith*, Fall, 22.

Caron, A.F. 1998. *Mothers and daughters: Searching for new connections*. New York: Henry Holt and Company.

Carothers, S. 1998. Catching the sense: Learning from our mothers to be Black and female. In *Families in the U.S.: Kinship and domestic politics*, ed. K.V. Hansen and A.I. Garey, 315–28. Philadelphia: Temple University Press.

Carter, E. 1996. Interview with Faith Sullivan. *Minnesota Monthly*, October, 24.

Chernin, K. 1985. *The hungry self: Women, eating, and identity*. New York: Times Books.

Chishti, S.H.M. 1991. *The book of Sufi healing*. Rochester, Vt.: Inner Traditions International.

Colette. 1966. *Earthly paradise: An autobiography*. Translated by Robert Phelps. New York: Farrar, Straus, and Giroux.

Colwin, L. 1988. *Home cooking*. New York: Alfred A. Knopf.

———. 1993. *More home cooking*. New York: HarperCollins Publishers.

Coontz, S. 1997. *The way we really are: Coming to terms with America's changing families*. New York: Basic Books.

Cooper, A. 1998. *"A woman's place is in the kitchen": The evolution of women chefs*. New York: Van Nostrand Reinhold.

Counihan, C., and P. Van Esterik, eds. 1997. *Food and culture: A reader*. New York: Routledge.

Cowan, R.S. 1982. The "Industrial Revolution" in the home: Household technology and social change in the twentieth century. In *Women's America: Refocusing the past*, ed. L.K. Kerber and J.D. Mathews, 324–38. New York: Oxford University Press.

Csikszentmihalyi, M. 1997. *Finding flow: The psychology of engagement with everyday life*. New York: Basic Books.

Curtin, D.W. and L.M. Heldke, eds. 1992. *Cooking, eating, thinking: Transformative philosophies of food*. Bloomington, Ind.: Indiana University Press.

Danforth, P. 2000. An urban Ojibwe wake, August 1999. Unpublished manuscript, Metropolitan State University, Minneapolis/St. Paul, Minnesota.

Daniel, J.L., and M. Effinger. 1996. Bosom biscuits: A study of African American intergenerational communication. *Journal of Black Studies* 27(2):183–200.

Darden, N.J., and C. Darden. 1978. *Spoonbread and strawberry wine: Recipes and reminiscences of a family*. Garden City, N.Y.: Anchor Press.

Dean, L.S. 1997. Memories of Mom. *Star Tribune*, 7 May, Taste section, T1-T2.

———. 1998a. Readers share their tales of 'Joy'. *Star Tribune*, 18 March, Taste section, T1, T6.

———. 1998b. A feast of love. *Star Tribune*, 6 May, Taste section, T1,4.

———. 1999a. Betty Crocker Kitchens chief retires—to cook. *Star Tribune*, 20 January, Taste section, T1.

———. 1999b. Her goal: Getting us back to dinner table. *Star Tribune*, 27 May, Taste section, T2.

de Certeau, M., L. Giard, and P. Mayol. 1998. *Practice of everyday life*, Vol. 2, *Living and cooking*, edited by L. Giard, translated by T.J. Tomasik. Minneapolis: University of Minnesota Press.

Debold, E., M. Wilson, and I. Malave. 1993. *Mother daughter revolution: From betrayal to power*. New York: Addison-Wesley.

Demos, J. 1986. *Past, present, and personal: The family and the life course in American history*. New York: Oxford University Press.

DePass, D. 1998. Author Maya Angelou tells Twin Cities women to cut new path. *Star Tribune*, 9 May, 4.

De Silva, C., ed. 1996. *In memory's kitchen: A legacy from the women of Terezín*, translated by B.S. Brown. Northvale, N.J.: Jason Aronson.

De Turenne, V. 1996. The family dinner. *Star Tribune*, 24 January, Taste section, T1, 2 *(Los Angeles Daily News)*.

DeVault, M.L. 1991. *Feeding the family: The social organization of caring as gendered work*. Chicago: The University of Chicago Press.

———. 1998. Affluence and poverty in feeding the family. In *Families in the U.S.: Kinship and domestic politics*, ed. K. Hansen and A.I. Garey, 171–88. Philadelphia: Temple University Press.

Doherty, W.J. 1997. *The intentional family: How to build family ties in our modern world*. Reading, Mass.: Addison-Wesley.

Douglas, M.M. 1994. *Eggs in the coffee, sheep in the corn: My 17 years as a farmwife*. St. Paul: Minnesota Historical Society Press.

Dreyer, C.A., and A.S. Dreyer. 1973. Family dinner time as a unique behavior habitat. *Family Process* 12:291–301.

Durbin, B. 1997. Making 'Joy' was no joy—kitchen had a lot of heat. *Star Tribune*, 19 March, Taste section, T5.

Eckstein, E.F. 1980. *Food, people, and nutrition*. Westport, Conn.: AVI Publishing Company, Inc.

Egerton, J. 1987. *Southern food: At home, on the road, in history*. New York: Alfred A. Knopf, Inc.

Ehrlich, E. 1997. *Miriam's kitchen*. New York: Viking.

Ellis, J. 1996. Fireworks and family fun. *House Beautiful*, July, 102–105.

Esquivel, L. 1989. *Like water for chocolate*. Translated by C. Christensen and T. Christensen. New York: Doubleday.

Faragher, J.M. 1982. The Midwestern farming family 1850. In *Women's America: Refocusing the past*, ed. L.K. Kerber and J.D. Mathews, 114–29. New York: Oxford University Press.

Farb, P., and G. Armelagos. 1980. *Consuming passions: The anthropology of eating*. Boston: Houghton Mifflin Company.

Fischer, L.R. 1986. *Linked lives*. New York: Harper and Row.

Footnotes. 1996. *Chronicle of Higher Education*, 25 October, A12.

Forster, R., and O. Ranum, eds. 1979. *Food and drink in history: Selections from the Annales Economies, Sociétés, Civilization*, Vol. 5. Translated by E. Forster and P.M. Ranum. Baltimore: The Johns Hopkins University Press.

Franklin, J. 1996. Food for 50: Second Sunday dinners build sense of community. *Minnesota Women's Press*, 29 May–11 June, 13.

Fuchs, N.K. 1989. *My mother made me do it: How your mother influenced your eating patterns—and how you can change them*. Los Angeles: Lowell House.

Future Homemakers updates name. 1999. *Star Tribune*, 7 July, A4 (Associated Press).

Galinsky, E. 1999a. *Ask the children: What America's children really think about working parents*. New York: William Morrow and Company, Inc.

———. 1999b. Do Working Parents Make the Grade? *Newsweek*, 30 August, 5 pp. Viewed on Academic Search Elite database (EBSCOHOST).

Garcia, C. 1997. *The Agüero sisters*. New York: Alfred A. Knopf.

Gillis, J.R. 1996. *A world of their own making: Myth, ritual, and the quest for family values*. New York: Basic Books.

Gillman, M.W., S.L. Rifas-Shiman, A.L. Frazier, H.R.H. Rockett, C.A. Camargo, Jr., A.E. Field, C.S. Berkey, and G.A. Colditz. 2000. Family dinner and diet quality among older children and adolescents. *Archives of Family Medicine* 9:235–40.

Glazer, N. 1980. Everyone needs three hands: Doing unpaid and paid work. In *Women and household labor*, ed. S.F. Berk, 249–74. Beverly Hills: Sage Publications.

Glickman, R. 1993. *Daughters of feminists*. New York: St. Martin's Press.

Gold, V.R., T.L. Hoyt, Jr., S.H. Ringe, S.B. Thistlethwaite, B.H. Throckmorton, Jr., and B.A. Withers, eds. 1995. *The New Testament and Psalms: An inclusive version*. New York: Oxford University Press.

Goldfein, J. 1994. *My cookbook: Recipes I have known and loved, Part I*. Privately printed.

Grimes, M. 1996. *Hotel Paradise*. New York: Ballantine Books.

Habeeb, V.T., and the food staff of *American Home*. 1966. *American Home all-purpose cookbook*. New York: M. Evans and Company.

Han, S. 1998. These moms can dish it out. *New York Daily News*, 6 May, Food Section, 3.

Heldke, L.M. 1992. Recipes for theory making. In *Cooking, eating, thinking: Transformative philosophies of food*, ed. D.W. Curtin and L.M. Heldke, 251–65. Bloomington, Ind.: Indiana University Press.

Hochschild, A.R., with A. Machung. 1998. The working wife as urbanizing peasant. In *Families in the U.S.: Kinship and domestic politics*, ed. K. Hansen and A.I. Garey, 779–90. Philadelphia: Temple University Press.

Holiday memories: Minnesota celebrities share their favorite holiday treasures. 1996. *Star Tribune*, 8 November, Holiday gift guide, 26–27.

Holmgren, K. 1998. Some holiday traditions change, but mother's Scandinavian krumkake endures. *Star Tribune*, 26 November, A45.

How I did it. 1998. *Essence*, June, 56.

Hudnut-Beumler, R. 1999. Eating the faith: Food and religion in the Protestant mainline. Interview with Daniel Sack. Material History of American Religion Project. Available from www.materialreligion.org (obtained October 29, 1999).

Hughes, M.H. 1997. Soul, Black women, and food. In *Food and culture: A reader*, ed. C. Counihan and P. Van Esterik, 272–80. New York: Routledge.

Hull, G.T. 1989. *Healing heart: 1973–1988*. Brooklyn, N.Y.: Kitchen Table: Women of Color Press.

Iggers, J. 1998. He tooled up American kitchens for French food. *Star Tribune*, 10 June, Taste section, T1–2.

Khan, H.I. 1991. *The mysticism of sound and music*. Rockport, Mass.: Element.

Laufer, P.D. 1989. Powerful and powerless: Paradox in Vivian Gornick's *Fierce Attachments*. In *Mother puzzles*, ed. M. Pearlman, 123–30. Westport, Conn.: Greenwood Press.

Lawrence-Lightfoot, S. 1994. *I've known rivers: Lives of loss and liberation*. New York: Addison Wesley.

Leeson, J.T. 1999. Cast-iron cookware outlives the cook. *Star Tribune*, 30 September, Taste section, T7.

Lightfoot, S.L. [S. Lawrence-Lightfoot]. 1988. *Balm in Gilead: Journey of a healer.* New York: Addison-Wesley.

*Like water for chocolate.* 1992. Produced and directed by A. Arau, screenplay by J. Esquivel. New York: Miramax Films.

Loeb, M.B. 1951. The social functions of food habits. *Journal of the American Academy of Applied Nutrition* 4:227–29

Lowinsky, N.R. 1992. *Stories from the motherline: Reclaiming the mother-daughter bond, finding our feminine souls.* Los Angeles: Jeremy P. Tarcher, Inc.

Manton, C. 1999. *Fed up: Women and food in America.* Westport, Conn.: Bergin & Garvey.

Marcus, J. 1996. Serving up food and vocabulary. *Times Educational Supplement,* 2 February, 15.

Martha Stewart is closing in on deal to gain more control over her empire. 1996. *Star Tribune,* 21 May, D10 (Associated Press).

Mason, B.A. 1999. *Clear Springs: A memoir.* New York: Random House.

Maynard, J. 1995. Pie baker's product explodes in oven and on paper. *All Things Considered,* 4 April. National Public Radio, transcript 1807–11, obtained through LEXIS-NEXIS, Academic Universe database.

Meier, P. 1997. Inheriting memories. *Star Tribune,* 2 March, E1,4.

Mellin, L.M., C.E. Irwin, and S. Scully. 1992. Prevalence of disordered eating in girls: A survey of middle-class children. *Journal of the American Dietetic Association* 92:851–53.

Mennell, S., Murcott, A., and A.H. van Otterloo. 1992. *The sociology of food: Eating, diet and culture.* Newbury Park, Calif.: Sage Publications.

Meyers, M. 1999. "A bite off Mama's plate": An exploration of mothers' and daughters' connections through food, manuscript submitted for a collection of articles on mothers and daughters, under preparation and tentatively titled *Mother-daughter communication: Voices from the professions,* A. Deakins and R.B. Lockridge, eds.

Miller, D.T. 1990. The impact of mothers' employment on the family meal. *Journal of Home Economics* 8(Spring):25–26, 56–57.

Mintz, S.W. 1996. *Tasting food, tasting freedom: Excursions into eating, culture, and the past.* Boston: Beacon Press.

Mintz, S., and S. Kellogg. (1988). *Domestic revolutions: A social history of American family life.* New York: The Free Press.

Murcott, A. 1983. Cooking and the cooked: A note on the domestic preparation of meals. In *The sociology of food and eating: Essays on the social significance of food,* ed. A. Murcott, 178–85. Aldershot, Hants, England: Gower.

*My dinner with André.* 1982. Produced by G.W. George and B. Karp and directed by L. Malle. Carmel, Calif.: Pacific Arts Video Records.

National Restaurant Association. 1997a. Restaurant spending survey. Press release on *Restaurant Spending Consumer Expenditure Survey,* 24 February. Washington, D.C.: National Restaurant Association.

———. 1997b. Frequent dinner customers: Who eats out and why. Press release on *The Frequent Dinner Customer,* 14 October. Washington, D.C.: National Restaurant Association.

———. 1997c. Table service trends—1997. Press release on *Table Service Trends— 1997*, 11 November. Washington, D.C.: National Restaurant Association.

Neidorf, R. 1996. Will work for food. *Minnesota Women's Press*, 29 May–11 June, 1, 6–7.

Neisser, E. 1967. *Mothers and daughters: A lifelong relationship*. New York: Harper and Row.

Neth, M. 1995. *Preserving the family farm: Women, community, and the foundations of agribusiness in the Midwest, 1900–1940*. Baltimore: The Johns Hopkins University Press.

Newman, L. 1993. *Eating our hearts out: Personal accounts of women's relationship to food*. Freedom, Calif.: Crossing Press.

Newport, F. 1997, March 19. Parenting has changed little in last 50 years, Gallup poll finds. *Star Tribune*, 19 March, E4.

Ng, M. 1998. *Eating Chinese food naked*. New York: Scribner.

Nice, V.E. 1992. *Mothers and daughters: The distortion of a relationship*. New York: St. Martin's Press.

North, B.B. 1993. *Vicky Giger's food favorites*. Privately printed.

Olsen, T., ed. 1984. *Mother to daughter, daughter to mother, mothers on mothering: A daybook and reader*. Old Westbury, N.Y.: Feminist Press.

Paul, M. 1998. Cooking up a plan to have family time. *Chicago Tribune*, 23 August, Section 13, 1.

Payne, K., ed. 1983. *Between ourselves: Letters between mothers and daughters 1750– 1982*. Boston: Houghton Mifflin.

Perkins, M. 1996. Profile: Kava Zabawa. *Minnesota Women's Press*, 29 May–11 June, 1, 23.

Phill, D.T. 1996a. Best of show. *Star Tribune*, 21 August, Taste section, T1–2.

———. 1996b. A happy cook makes for happy food—try to avoid mad cooking. *Star Tribune*, 8 September, E2.

———. 1997a. In kitchen with three good cooks, trays of food are natural result. *Star Tribune*, 17 August, E3.

———. 1997b. Wedding-gift recipe collection grows into a family cookbook. *Star Tribune*, 30 November, E3.

———. 1998. Putting recipes together brings her friends and family together. *Star Tribune*, 28 June, E3.

———. 1999a. Marilyn Stillman received gift: Her mother gave her the chance to help in the kitchen with her grandmother. *Star Tribune*, 25 March, Taste section, T4.

———. 1999b. Her travels provide inspiration and source for recipes. *Star Tribune*, 3 June, Taste section, T8.

Pomerantz, K. 1998, Fall. Culinary connections: Food for the soul. *The United Synagogue Review*, 8–10.

Pope, H.G., J.I. Hudson, D. Yurgelun-Todd, and M. Hudson. 1984. Prevalence of anorexia nervosa and bulimia in three student populations. *International Journal of Eating Disorders* 3 (3):45–51.

Prior-Nolan, P. 2000. Wedge's Foley wins top honor. *Star Tribune*, 27 July, Taste section, T3.

Reichl, R. 1998. *Tender at the bone: Growing up at the table.* New York: Random House.

Remen, R.N. 1996. *Kitchen table wisdom: Stories that heal.* New York: Riverhead.

Roberts, C. 1998. *We are our mothers' daughters.* New York: William Morrow & Company, Inc.

Roberts, K. 1999. "Moms" make mealtime connection. *Star Tribune,* 27 May, Taste section, T3.

Roberts, S.B., and M.B. Heyman, with L. Tracy. 1999. *Feeding your child for lifelong health.* New York: Bantam Books.

Robinson, J.P. 1980. Housework technology and household work. In *Women and household labor,* ed. S.F. Berk, 53–68. Beverly Hills: Sage Publications.

Robison, S.H. 1997. The joy of eating. *More,* Spring, 114–16, 18, 20.

Rollins, J. 1990. Review of *Domesticity and dirt: Housewives and domestic servants in the United States, 1920–1945. Sage* 7(1, Summer):76.

Rombauer, I.S., M.R. Becker, and E. Becker. 1997. *The joy of cooking.* New York: Scribner.

Rosen, M.J., ed. 1996. *Food fight: Poets join the fight against hunger with poems to favorite foods.* New York: Harcourt Brace & Company.

Rossi, A.S. 1995. Commentary: Alternative theory and analysis modes. In *Adult intergenerational relations: Effects of societal change,* ed. V.L. Bengtson, K.W. Schaie and L.M. Burton, 264–76. New York: Springer Publishing Company.

Sack, D. 1999. On deciphering a potluck: The social meaning of church socials. Material History of American Religion Project. Available from *www. materialreligion.org* (obtained October 29, 1999).

Schloff, L.M. 1996. *"And prairie dogs weren't kosher": Jewish women and the Upper Midwest since 1855.* St. Paul: Minnesota Historical Society Press.

Schor, J.B. 1998. Time squeeze: The extra month of work. In *Families in the U.S.: Kinship and domestic politics,* ed. K.V. Hansen and A.I. Garey, 113–30. Philadelphia: Temple University Press.

Selingo, J. 1999, July 30. How food and memory come together. *The Chronicle of Higher Education,* A7.

Shacochis, B. 1994. *Domesticity: A gastronomic interpretation of love.* New York: Charles Scribner's Sons.

Shakur, A., and J. Chesimard. 1978. Women in prison: How we are. *Black Scholar* 9(7):8–15.

Sherline, R. 1993. *Letters home: Celebrated authors write to their mothers.* New York: Timken.

Sicherman, A. 1999. Apple pie and love: Recipes from Mom. *Star Tribune,* 6 May, Taste section, T1, 6–7.

Sklar, D. 1996. Passing away. In *Our mothers ourselves: Writers and poets celebrating motherhood,* ed. K.J. Donnelly and J.B. Bernstein, 115–17. Westport, Conn.: Bergin & Garvey.

Smart-Grosvenor, V.M. 1992. From *Vibration cooking: Or the travel notes of a Geechee girl.* In *Cooking, eating, thinking: Transformative philosophies of food,* ed. D.W.

Curtin and L.M. Heldke, 295–97. Bloomington, Ind.: Indiana University Press.

Smith, L. 1962. *Memory of a large Christmas*. New York: W.W. Norton.

Smith-Rosenberg, C. 1985. *Disorderly conduct: Visions of gender in Victorian America*. New York: Oxford University Press.

*Soul food*. 1997. Written and directed by G. Tillman, Jr., produced by T.E. Edmonds and R. Teitel. Beverly Hills, Calif.: Fox 2000 Pictures.

Spruill, J.C. 1982. Housewives and their helpers. In *Women's America: Refocusing the past*, ed. L.K. Kerber and J.D. Mathews, 26–36. New York: Oxford University Press.

Stack, C. 1974. *All our kin: Strategies for survival in a Black community*. New York: Harper & Row.

Story, M., K. Rosenwinkel, J.H. Himes, M. Resnick, L.J. Harris, and R.W. Blum. 1991. Demographic and risk factors associated with chronic dieting in adolescents. *American Journal of Diseases of Children* 145:994–98.

Sutel, S. 1999. New flavor at *Gourmet* magazine. *Star Tribune*, 18 August, E1, E7 (Associated Press).

Taylor, J. 1990. *Grace Paley: Illuminating the dark lives*. Austin: University of Texas Press.

Thorson, D.T.P. 1996a. Like Mother, like chef. *Star Tribune*, 8 May, Taste section, T1.

———. 1996b. Bread baker insists on fresh ingredients and premium taste. *Star Tribune*, 7 July, E3.

Tilly, L.A., and J.W. Scott. 1987. *Women, work, and family*. New York: Methuen.

Tisdale, S. 2000. *The best thing I ever tasted: The secret of food*. New York: Riverhead Books.

Uhlenberg, P. 1995. Commentary: Demographic influences on intergenerational relationships. In *Adult intergenerational relations: Effects of societal change*, ed. V.L. Bengtson, K.W. Schaie and L.M. Burton, 19–25. New York: Springer Publishing Company.

Vanek, J. 1980. Household work, wage work, and sexual equality. In *Women and household labor*, ed. S.F. Berk, 275–92. Beverly Hills: Sage Publications.

Wade-Gayles, G. 1991. Connected to Mama's spirit. In *Double stitch: Black women write about mothers and daughters*, ed. P. Bell-Scott, B. Guy-Sheftall, J. Jones Royster, J. Sims-Wood, M. DeCosta-Willis, and L. Fultz, 214–38. Boston: Beacon Press.

Walker, A. 1983. In search of our mothers' gardens. In *In search of our mothers' gardens*, 231–43. New York: Harcourt Brace Jovanovich.

———. 1997. My mother's blue bowl. In *Anything we love can be saved*, 217–220. New York: Random House.

Walker, J.A. 1996. Letters in the attic: Private reflections of women, wives, and mothers. *Marriage and Family Review* 24:105–21. Published simultaneously in M.B. Sussman and J.F. Gilgun, eds., *The methods and methodologies of qualitative family research*, 9–40. New York: Haworth, Inc.

Walker, R. 1998, May 7. Mother's day: Forming a bond in the kitchen. *The Atlanta Journal and Constitution*, Food section, 1H.

Waterhouse, D. 1997. *Like mother, like daughter*. New York: Hyperion Books.

Webb, A. 1997. Keepers of the flame: Farming women across the Midwest frontier 1840–1910. Unpublished manuscript, Metropolitan State University, Minneapolis/St. Paul, Minnesota.

Whirlpool Foundation. 1998, May. Summary of *Report card on the new providers*, available from *www.whirlpoolcorp.com*, foundation link.

White, B. 1993. *Mama makes up her mind*. Reading, Mass.: Addison-Wesley.

Wilbur, S. 1998, October 28-November 10. Kneading time: Karen Franzmeier cooks up peace and justice. *Minnesota Women's Press*, 1, 12.

Wilgocki, V. 1996, May 29-June 11. Warm and chewy: Happy food memories stir a woman's soul. *Minnesota Women's Press*, 9.

Williams, G., III. 1995, October 29. 'Soulful' eating is an aid to the body and spirit. *Star Tribune*, E1, 7 (reprint from *Longevity Magazine*).

Willits, M.G. 1996, November 13. Cherished cookware is making new memories. *Star Tribune*, Taste section, T1–2.

Willoughby, J. 1995, May 10. Feminists find history in the kitchen. *The New York Times*, C4.

Winter, O. 1965. Vesta, a modern woman. *Mountain Life and Work* 45, 31–32.

Wyman, W.D. 1972. *Frontier woman: The life of a woman homesteader on the Dakota frontier*. River Falls: University of Wisconsin-River Falls Press.

Yezierska, A. 1975. *Bread givers*. New York: Persea Books.

Yoshimoto, B. 1988. *Kitchen*. New York: Grove Press.

# Index

## About the Author

MIRIAM MEYERS spent her childhood in Atlanta, Georgia, where her mother worked in the food service industry for four decades. Since completing degrees in English, French, and linguistics at Peabody College, Vanderbilt University and Georgetown University, Miriam has taught and worked as a writer, editor, and administrator. She is currently Professor of Literature and Language at Metropolitan State University in Minnesota, where she has specialized in language and gender for two decades. She lives in Minneapolis, where she gardens and watches birds when she is not writing and teaching.